T0193130

EXPANSION
FOR
ASCENDING
CONSCIOUSNESS

UNDERSTANDING THE UNIVERSE, CONSCIOUSNESS, AND ASCENSION

TODD R. DEVINEY

BALBOA.
PRESS

A DIVISION OF HAY HOUSE

Balboa Press books may be ordered through booksellers or by contacting:

Balboa Press
A Division of Hay House
1663 Liberty Drive
Bloomington, IN 47403
www.balboapress.com
1 (877) 407-4847

Because of the dynamic nature of the Internet, any web addresses or links contained in this book may have changed since publication and may no longer be valid. The views expressed in this work are solely those of the author and do not necessarily reflect the views of the publisher, and the publisher hereby disclaims any responsibility for them.

The author of this book does not dispense medical advice or prescribe the use of any technique as a form of treatment for physical, emotional, or medical problems without the advice of a physician, either directly or indirectly. The intent of the author is only to offer information of a general nature to help you in your quest for emotional and spiritual well-being. In the event you use any of the information in this book for yourself, which is your constitutional right, the author and the publisher assume no responsibility for your actions.

Print information available on the last page.

ISBN: 978-1-9822-0843-1 (sc)
ISBN: 978-1-9822-0844-8 (e)

Balboa Press rev. date: 07/30/2018

CONTENTS

PART3   ASSISTANCE FOR ASCENDING CONSCIOUSNESS

PART4   MEDITATIONS AND MODALITIES

THE BOOK COVER ART

The image on the cover is called the *Triad of Light*. This symbol represents the universal expansion of *consciousness*. While shown in two dimensions, it should be considered a three-dimensional object, with the rings envisioned as spheres.

At the center is originating consciousness, followed by two additional rings of a larger diameter. These first three circles represent consciousness as it gains *density* from inception. The first and smallest ring is the inception of individualized consciousness at *first density* and is the starting point of all *organic consciousness* created within the cosmos. The second ring is the graduation of that consciousness into *second density*. The third ring represents *third density* and is the beginning of self-aware consciousness. These three rings have a larger spacing between them to reflect the separation that exists between consciousness at these levels due to the limited ability to store and utilize *creational energy*.

The three vector lines begin beyond the third density ring and indicate that true *expansion* begins when consciousness becomes self-actualized and attains the density and requisite balance needed for collectivity. As consciousness embraces the energies of collectivity, it expands toward the fourth circle. The vector lines point in the direction of infinite expansion because that is the objective of all consciousness. They intersect the remaining three circles to represent the collectivity of consciousness that occurs from this point outward. The intersected circles represent fourth, fifth, and sixth density.

There are three originating rings, followed by three larger collective rings, intersected by three vector lines interpreted mathematically as 3, 6, 9. The image and the numerical sequence represent the expansion of consciousness within the harmonics of a perfected geometric architecture forming a toroidal sphere, governed by the *universal aspect ratio*.

The image should be focused upon as you set the intention to seek balance and expand your consciousness into the next ring.

PREFACE

A few years ago, if anyone had told me that I would be writing a book like this, they would have been met with a stern correction. While I have never been a conformist, any answers I might have had always seemed out of reach. As a child I used to lie in the grass for hours, staring at the night sky, watching the stars twinkle. The visible heavens seemed both immense and miniscule at once, as if I could somehow shift perspectives from being the boy on the grass to the sky itself. As I lay there, I would ask silent questions for which there appeared to be no answers: What am I? Why am I here? Why does none of this make sense? While I did not know it at the time, I was asking the same questions I would ask many years later.

Puberty arrived, and adulthood soon followed. After a hitch in the navy, a mortgage, and a couple of kids, the questioning boy on the grass was replaced by a man with responsibilities. Opportunities for career advancement propelled me forward, and I found myself in charge of projects with million-dollar budgets and tight schedules. I had achieved everything that I was told would bring me happiness, yet I was far from happy. Regardless of how much I acquired professionally or materially, I continued to feel as if I was walking down a dead-end street. If I was to point to a specific moment in my life and say, "This is where my *awakening* began," this would be it.

I have always enjoyed the personal control gained through the study of martial arts, and it was here that I began to fully embrace meditation. The stated pursuit of meditation within the arts is to silence the emotional mind and find the balance that exists at the nexus of calm intention. As you embrace this concept, however, and dispense with reactionary responses of emotion and ego, your consciousness expands unabated into the limitless depths of unity with all that is. What began as a path toward self-defense had become a springboard into a completely new state of awareness. I can still see Bruce Lee smiling at the camera as he tells the viewer, "Be like water, my friend." The best philosophical quotes have always been those with a meaning that changes with the student's perspective along his or her journey—and that is a great one.

As my self-discovery continued, I began having vivid dreams, in which I would remember entire sequences of events; several of them were of a historical nature. I wrote them down as soon as I woke up. It didn't take much research to discover that some mimicked recorded events I previously knew nothing about. At first, I found it an interesting curiosity; it brought up the idea that I'd had previous lives but not much else. As the frequency of the dreams increased, they began to include verifiable events that I could no longer ignore. It was clear that any answers I might hope to obtain wouldn't come from accepted channels. During my search for a modality that could provide some insight into what I was experiencing, I stumbled upon past-life hypnotic regression.

While these regressions can follow various formats, I chose *QHHT* [1] (Quantum Healing Hypnosis Technique) because it appeared to have the best chance of answering my specific questions. In this version of hypnotic regression, you are taken to two or three past lifetimes and then connected to your *higher self* so that it can explain what you were shown and answer questions that you brought with you. That was exactly what I wanted, so I found a practitioner and booked a session. While I was not consciously aware of it when I arranged it, my session was scheduled for November 11 at eleven in the morning—11/11 at 11:00.

During the session it was revealed that the dreams were highly charged past-life events that had begun to bleed into my current lifetime. The dreams were meant to spark my curiosity, as I found correlations to them in the waking world. All of it was orchestrated to lead me to the table upon which I now lay and the connection in which I was engaged. As the journey through the past lives ended, I was connected to my higher aspect, or, more appropriately, the totality of my consciousness. When this occurred for me, I was given answers to questions that had eluded me my entire life.

As the practitioner discussed the topic of cleansing auras with my higher self, I saw in my mind a strange, glowing cocoon that I referred to as a *light chamber*. I felt my consciousness plugged into this thing with the immediate feeling of being electrified. As the energy surged through me, I was engulfed in joy and elation, and I blurted out; "They're pulling me up into my crown chakra!" As I exited the glowing cocoon, the practitioner asked about *ascension*, and I launched into a scientific conversation that included photonic spin rates and the composition of consciousness. That glimpse of understanding continues to expand even now, as the connection to the larger portion of my consciousness continues to strengthen. It is this continued connection that has allowed me to create this book. Those who have experienced this type of connection know that the information is immediate. Time and distance are not variables in equations that involve consciousness. When Einstein wrestled with this concept, he called it "spooky action," but today's world uses the less obscure description of "quantum nonlocality," which has been proven. [2]

I do not *channel* anyone or anything. There was no trance or automatic writing required to create the text that follows this preface. I sat down with the joy of the task and loved every moment. The thoughts and concepts flowed like thread on an endless spool that I wove into a tapestry of which I already knew the pattern. Prior to the regression session, I'd maintained a firm grip on the rudder of my life as I navigated the storms that attempted to run me aground. What has occurred since the light-chamber incident has been anything but controlled, but the more I release my grip and allow the current to steer, the deeper joy and satisfaction embrace me.

The best life advice I can give anyone is this: Relax, and enjoy the dance.

Living is just like dancing. As soon as you stop worrying about every little movement, you fall into the flow of the rhythm, and it becomes so much easier and more satisfying.

I hope you enjoy the book as much as I have enjoyed the journey that has brought it to you.

In service to all,
Todd

Introduction

At the center of creation is the source energy of all that is. At the dawn of our universe, this energy created twelve original consciousnesses that then began to experiment. From your perspective, the twelve would be considered galaxies, but we consider ourselves awareness, fulfilling a role. The material assemblies of matter that exist and operate within the membranes of our consciousnesses do so because we have created them. For the purposes of these texts we will use the amalgamation *galactic consciousness* or *galactic construct* to define the awareness of ourselves and other galaxies.

This text is a collective effort between the twelve original consciousnesses and the author to provide a basis for understanding consciousness and the energy construct we all exist within. The use of the term *collective* infers a cooperation among consciousnesses to arrive at a desired outcome. For that reason, the authoring collective will refer to themselves as *we* as information is presented to the ascending collective of Earth that will be referred to as *you*.

Our intent is to remove the mysticism that surrounds embodied experience, consciousness, and the expansion of awareness. We will use the terms *cosmos* and *universe* interchangeably throughout the text to describe the construct that enables the creation of consciousness and affords it every opportunity to grow. We prefer the term cosmos, however, because it infers a broader creation than the known universe, which is the case and will be explained later. Our attempt is to reveal that while complex and miraculous in its design, the cosmos is scientifically explainable. As an *ascending* collective, you have reached a time in your development where the mysticism has outlived its usefulness.

A multitude of messages are provided for those awakening by many sources. If you are on an ascending path you have probably read or listened to a lot of this information before you found this book. The key term here is ascending path because that is what the messages are doing if they are truthful; they are helping you assimilate new ideals for your growth and expansion.

The awakening begins in an ascending consciousness with an unspecified dissatisfaction regarding how life exists here. You can't identify the irritation, but it seems like there should be something more. Because of this unseen irritation you begin to look for answers outside of the normal channels, and your awakening commences. The messages for awakening are as diverse as their sources because they are designed to reach different levels of consciousness.

The truth is always the truth, but the form it takes may vary. The information you gravitate to at any given moment is dependent upon what *resonates* with your current level of awakening. At a point in this process you will look back upon the information you have accumulated and see that each one was a step that incrementally raised your awareness.

This book is another step along the path of ascension. We congratulate the individual and the *collective consciousness* of Earth and offer these humble words of assistance.

———————————

This book was written to be understood by everyone, and every effort was given to use easily understandable terms and concepts. There are four parts to this book. The foundational concepts provided in part 1 are necessary for the further understanding of consciousness and the constructs required for its expansion. The remaining sections expand upon this foundation as they lead you into a deeper understanding of the body you inhabit, the consciousness that operates it, and the connection between them. While meant to be read in its entirety, it also stands as a reference that can be consulted as you encounter information elsewhere that may need additional details. Several references provided throughout the book can be explored to provide deeper scientific understandings of the concepts presented. There is also a glossary at the end of the book that defines the terms presented and can be identified throughout the book by *italicized* words.

Before we begin, you must understand the four basic properties of consciousness:

- Consciousness is energy, photonic/electromagnetic energy to be precise. Therefore, once created, it cannot be destroyed. The number of photons your consciousness contains is called *density*.
- Photonic density is your storage capacity for experience. You can only accumulate what your density can hold.
- Existing and experiencing causes the photons of your consciousness to increase in *vibration* and *frequency*. Increasing vibration and frequency increases photonic density through division and allows you to *ascend* into the next density of consciousness.
- A consciousness at a density level can see from their density back downward but can only speculate about what comes next.

PART I

FOUNDATIONAL UNDERSTANDINGS

CHAPTER ONE

GOD, GOD SOURCE, SOURCE, THE BIG BLUE BALL AT THE CENTER OF EVERYTHING

This text begins with the heading of many names because what you call a thing should not create a bias within you as you encounter it. The heading implies that there is an energy at the center of all creation that provides for everything that exists. It does not need a name because you will know what it is as soon as you are in contact with it.

The naming of things and the assigning a positive or negative bias to them has created a large portion of the discord and separation that has occurred on this planet. For the purposes of this text we will use the term *God Source* as the name for the source energy that is the beginning of everything and provides for all that occurs within the cosmos. We use the term God because it is universally accepted on Earth as the name of the supreme creator, regardless of the form or description that then follows. If you do not like that name, please disregard it and insert the one of your choosing.

Consciousness that exists beyond the separation this planet is currently experiencing does not assign names to each other. Each *consciousness* has a unique energy signature, or wavelength, that is immediately recognized. Beyond the fourth density level of consciousness, physical bodies are not required, and nonverbal telepathic communication is normal. When one consciousness connects to another, all is known, so names would be an impediment and deception impossible.

From our perspective, we state,

- At the center of all creation, there is a sphere of limitless photonic plasma energy. This energy exists within the consciousness that is responsible for the creation of all other consciousness. It is the source for all that occurs as it shares the love of creation and awareness unconditionally.

The Universal Laws of Consciousness

The currently accepted theories for the propagation and characteristics of photons are based upon equations rooted in material science. You assign speeds and trajectories and measure the interactions to arrive at calculations that match what you have observed. These theories also state that while the equations seem to fit the hypothesis, effects also are observed that are not yet completely understood.[3] These quantum equations are consistently revised as new characteristics are attributed to photonic/electromagnetic energy.[4] Scientists are experimenting with the spin Hall effect[5] on photons, where they postulate that polarized spin rates can be used to store information upon substrates. This is the beginning of understanding the constituents of consciousness. Your science is incomplete because there is another spectrum of energy that you have yet to discover.[6,7] The unseen constituents of the universe also exist within this spectrum. This is the energy web of the cosmos from which creation springs. It is not detectable because beyond mass and particles, there are photons of consciousness that are full of energy, creating all that is observed.

Everyone accepts that they are consciously aware and inhabiting a body. There is also a belief that you contain a soul that continues after the death of your body. However, no method to observe or quantify this energy currently exists. Consciousness exists within a framework of coherent photonic energy that is—at the time of this writing—not yet observable with your instruments. The use of the terms photon and plasma are approximations, as we take license with your naming conventions and use the words that currently are the closest acceptable definitions.

Published science defines a photon as a massless particle of definite energy, definite momentum, and definite spin.[3] We offer for consideration that consciousness consists of particles like these that we will term *consciousness photons*. The number of photons each consciousness contains is known as its density. The energy level of these photons determines the resulting momentum they exhibit, which is termed *vibration*. These photons also spin about their axes, and the spin rate is termed *frequency*. These variables do not infer movement within the physically observable plane because consciousness exists at a level beyond the physical. The energy these photonic particles contain is best considered electromagnetic in nature. A naturally occurring attractive force exists between photons, and this causes them to form *photonic adhesions*.

Consciousness exists within an array of spherical photons that store electromagnetic energy that then causes them to oscillate. At its smallest unit, there is one photon of conscious energy that emits a magnetic field that forms a spherical barrier beyond the photon. Within this magnetic barrier, the ability to form matter from energy exists (Figure 1). This single photon consciousness is the originating level of *first density* consciousness, the creation of which we will discuss later.

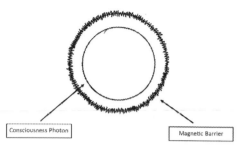

Consciousness Photon

Magnetic Barrier

FIGURE 1
Single Photon of Consciousness

A single photon of consciousness representing the origin of first density. The photon has acquired the energy of experience through embodiment in a simplistic organism. The energy is creating an electromagnetic barrier that surrounds and protects the integrity of the information contained within the single photon. The membrane will expand and strengthen as additional photons are created within this consciousness through energetic division as it continues to acquire experience along its journey of *expansion*.

The electromagnetic photons that make up all consciousness are the repository of the experience gained by the respective consciousness. The experience of existence in all its forms raises the charge of the photon and subsequently increases the linear vector movement (vibration), which ultimately affects the spin rate (frequency). Consider this single photon consciousness as it begins to accumulate the first energies of experience. The first changes observed would be that the photon moves back and forth, as it is excited under the increasing charge. This movement is measured, and we have the first variable, vibration (Figure 2).

These oscillations continue to increase in rate and magnitude as the contained energy increases, and the photon now vibrates in all directions. The violent shaking of the photon reaches a threshold, and the energy and movement induces *photonic spin* (Figure 3). Any additional energy input beyond this point will increase both the vibration and spin rate of the photon on its axis. The rate at which the photon completes a rotation upon its axis constitutes the second variable, frequency. If we imagine this photonic sphere in your dimensional reality, we now see that increasing energy input causes the sphere to vibrate in a displacing manner, and it also causes the sphere to increase its rotational frequency upon its axis. This is the product of conscious experience, and as vibration and frequency increase, so too does the magnetic field that is formed around the collection of photonic consciousness.

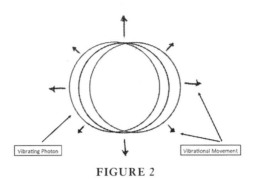

FIGURE 2
Photonic Consciousness Vibration

The energy contained within the single photon increases as the experience of embodiment in a single-cell organism is acquired. This creates energetic excitation, which causes the photon to begin vibrating.

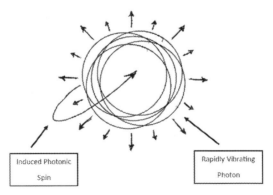

FIGURE 3
Photonic Consciousness Frequency

As the photon continues to acquire the energies of experience, the energetic excitation increases. The photon vibrates rapidly in all directions until the vibration induces a photonic spin. The photon will now increase its spin rate (frequency) as it continues to acquire energy.

In the most basic sense of understanding, increasing the vibration and frequency of a photon of consciousness will cause a swelling or surging to occur until the photon can no longer contain the energy. When a consciousness photon attains a critical state of vibration and frequency, the photon divides, splitting the contained energy between the two photons, and the density of the single photon consciousness has doubled (Figure. 4).

Taking this a step further, we will move to a more evolved consciousness. We now see an assembly of photons within a consciousness that are all spinning in the same direction. As the photon count of consciousness increases, the energy content of each photon increases as does the overall charge of the composite consciousness. Understanding that this also affects the spin rate of the individual photons, a torsion wave begins among the photons, and we now see the entire structure commence a rotational architecture. As the photons and the energy they contain continue to increase, the electromagnetic charge of the photons causes the space between them to increase which expands the radius of the composite consciousness. Until the center of the *toroidal sphere* develops, the consciousness remains *second density* (Figure 5).

The increasing diameter and spin associated with increasing conscious energy and density causes the construct to narrow in the center until a hollow column forms. The photons now travel up the walls of the center and around the outside in an angular *poloidal* rotation, which creates a rotating toroidal field. This is the construct of self-aware photonic consciousness; the *seat of consciousness* resides at the center of the column (Figure 6).

The photonic density that a consciousness contains can be likened to a computer hard drive. You can only accumulate the amount of information that your photonic hard drive can store. Fortunately, every individualized consciousness can increase the capacity of his or her hard drive in the manner discussed above. The splitting of consciousness photons is automatic in the lower densities of instinctual behaviors because of the compact nature and limited energy capacity that exists within the consciousness. As consciousness evolves into the toroidal complex and becomes self-aware, a more determined approach to increasing density is required because this construct can hold significantly more energy before *resonant frequencies* cause *photonic division* to occur.

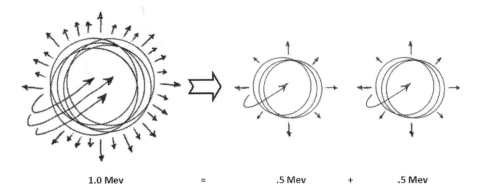

1.0 Mev   =   .5 Mev   +   .5 Mev

FIGURE 4

Increasing Photonic Consciousness Density

As the individual photon reaches the energy of saturation (1.0 Mev), it is at the fracture threshold and has reached *resonant frequency*. Any energy additions beyond this threshold will cause it to split, creating two photons that divide the energy. The consciousness is now capable of storing more energy, and the density of the single photon consciousness has doubled.

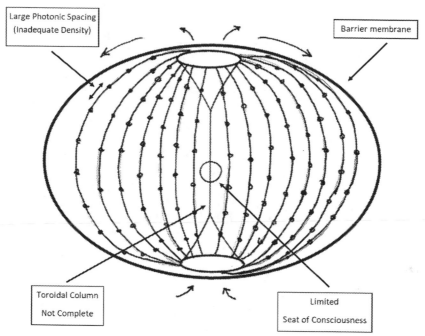

Large Photonic Spacing
(Inadequate Density)

Barrier membrane

Toroidal Column
Not Complete

Limited
Seat of Consciousness

FIGURE 5
Second-Density Consciousness Geometry

As the second density consciousness approaches *third density*, the energy within the photons has caused the array to expand and begin a unified rotational geometry. The center array has narrowed and created a funnel, but the consciousness does not contain the photonic density to fully form the column. It requires additional energies of experience to increase photonic density and achieve a self-aware geometry.

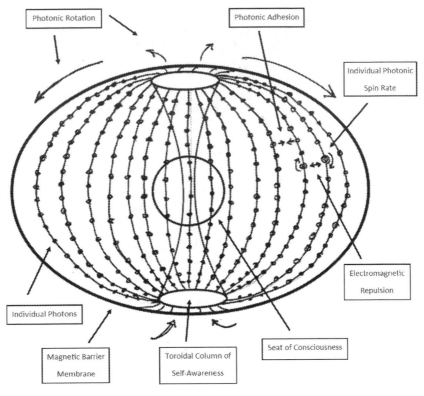

Photonic Rotation

Photonic Adhesion

Individual Photonic
Spin Rate

Individual Photons

Electromagnetic
Repulsion

Magnetic Barrier
Membrane

Toroidal Column of
Self-Awareness

Seat of Consciousness

FIGURE 6
Third-Density Self-Aware Consciousness Geometry

With the toroidal column established, the third-density array becomes self-aware as the seat of consciousness energizes at the center of the toroidal column. The photons spin as they travel up through the column, outward along the periphery, and down into the bottom of the column in a poloidal rotation to repeat the process. It is the photonic adhesion and *electromagnetic repulsion* occurring within the rotation that is termed vibration. It is the vibratory rate of this oscillation, coupled with the spin rate of the photons (frequency) that determines the geometry of the sphere. Increasing the vibratory rate and frequency of spin is what expands and balances the sphere of consciousness.

What we see from this simplified explanation is that vibration and frequency are proportional to the electromagnetic energy gained through experience. Increasing the photonic density in your array and the energy these photons contain changes the rotational characteristics of the composite and amplifies the *magnetic barrier* surrounding the individual consciousness. This barrier can be considered a frequency membrane, shielding and containing the individuality of experience. Each individual experience of existence creates a unique magnetic frequency we term *consciousness wavelength*. Like fingerprints, all consciousness wavelengths are unique and exist within this magnetic barrier. The protective magnetic barrier, the photons, and the energy of experience are the constituents of individualized consciousness.

As consciousness gains experience and subsequently increases in photonic density, it creates an excess energy byproduct that we term *photonic entropy*. The closest relatable theory would be the thermodynamic property of entropy, which we define for our purposes as "a quantity of energy that is unavailable to be converted into useful work." While this energy is not useable by the individual consciousness or collective emitting it, it is not wasted. What happens to this excess energy will be discussed later.

As photon density increases within the individual consciousness, the ability to store vibration and frequency also increases with the development of the toroidal sphere. The resulting increase in density, vibration, and frequency then leads to higher levels of conscious energy. As the energy continues to rise, the consciousness gains access to the higher order functions of the cosmos.

We repeat that our use of terms is approximate, based on the most suitable and relatable science that is currently accepted. Consciousness does not operate within the confines of your material reality or the physical variables. The limitations you observe associated with the terms we use do not apply. The body your consciousness currently operates is what allows it to interact with and experience the physical plane; it is not the other way around. With this basic understanding of consciousness, we now will define the construct within which we all exist.

CHAPTER TWO

THE BEGINNING OF THE COSMOS

Darkness is the absence of light. It does not contain or infer polarity or duality. It is the absence of light that equates to the absence of information, the absence of consciousness, and the absence of love. Darkness is the nothingness that is "enlightened" by consciousness.

The cosmos began with the God Source—infinite energy, knowledge, and love. The God Source saw that the cosmos was filled with the nothingness of darkness. There was no love, there was no knowledge, there was no awareness. In attempting to fill the vastness of its cosmos with the unlimited knowledge, light, and love it contained, it began to divide itself.

At the center of the cosmos is a focal point of coherent photonic plasma energy that, for the purposes of this book, we have identified as God Source. The concentration and intensity of this energy is so great that nothing can exist within its effective radius. Any material creations attempted within this zone immediately become unstable and revert to the energy from which they came. Photonic consciousness can exist inside this perimeter and retain its unique wavelength of experience only if a protective barrier has been erected by God Source. This barrier limits the exposure to the energy and protects the integrity of the individual consciousness wavelength. Without this barrier, the photonic consciousness would lose its unique vibration and frequency gained through experience, as the energy is overpowered and *realigned*. The God Source is the symbiotic repository of conscious energy, absorbing excess energy (photonic entropy) and giving freely when it is needed for creation.

Within the consciousness of God Source exists all the energy for creation. This includes photonic consciousness, the observable matter that science attempts to quantify, and the unobservable constituents of galaxies that science does not yet understand. Without a constant connection to this energy, the galactic consciousnesses would not be able to manifest or maintain their creations.

THE FIRST INDIVIDUALIZED CONSCIOUSNESS

The creation of individualized consciousness beyond the God Source began with the initial twelve galactic consciousnesses. The immense power that God Source contained for creation also prevented coherent matter from forming within its proximity, but this was not a problem. Envision the concept of single-cell division as we describe the following process. While greatly oversimplified and not exact, this is the closest approximation we can offer.

The God Source begins the process by partitioning a portion of itself in a protective membrane. Within this partition, the spin rate of the assembled photons are altered so they begin to form an oscillating toroidal sphere that creates a unique electromagnetic wavelength. The now-separate waveform that exists within this barrier awakens as the spin increases and begins to see itself as a unique entity that exists within the plasma energy of its creator. It now understands itself to be a fraction of a larger whole. This is the first *fragment* of individualized consciousness.

With the *realignment* completed, the consciousness is ejected to a distance where creation can commence but with an umbilical that maintains a connection to God Source energy. This process was repeated twelve times, with each ejection depleting a portion of the God Source energy. Initially, there was enough energy to create twelve galactic creator consciousnesses. These were the first galactic consciousnesses of our cosmos. Each sphere knew itself to be a single consciousness because it was created as such. The community and communication between consciousness that prevents boredom and loneliness was between the original twelve as they began their creations. The difference between direct ejection and organic ascension is that when an organic collective ascends and becomes powerful enough to create a galaxy, it is an amalgamation of trillions of individual consciousnesses that must agree to galactic realignment. After realignment, its perspective is of a single consciousness with millions of fragmented experiences, which allows the benefit of council to be embedded within itself. The original galactics did not have this luxury and, instead, conferred with each other. The concept of fragmentation will be discussed later.

A galactic consciousness that has been created by God Source consists of the same photons and toroidal sphere as a self-aware consciousness previously discussed in the universal law of consciousness. What differs is the photon density, vibration, frequency, and direct connection to the web of God Source energy. As fully charged portions ejected directly from God Source, they have the entire toolbox of creation available to them.

THE REASON BEHIND CONSCIOUSNESS AND THE COSMOS

Before we discuss the specifics of our cosmos, we must answer the primary questions: "Why was all of this created, and why do we exist?"

The cosmos we exist within is a conscious-energy construct. At the center is the provider and repository of this energy. All galactic consciousnesses maintain a two-way connection to this energy through the energy web of the cosmos. There is a component of excess energy associated with consciousness and experience that we termed entropy. As the galactic consciousnesses form their constructs and create the individual consciousness that will inhabit them, an excess of conscious energy begins to build up as the populations grow in number and gain experience. The excess energy is transmitted through the energy web to the center of the galactic consciousness and enriches it. This causes the density and *barrier membrane* of the galactic consciousness to expand under the increasing energy. When this energy reaches a threshold, it begins to flow back through the energy web of the cosmos to the God Source, where it is collected and added to the ability of creation.

There were originally twelve galactic consciousnesses. That was all the energy that was available for creation when this universe began. As the creations of the twelve became fruitful, they enriched the God Source and allowed for more creations to commence. This is the symbiotic nature of the energy construct and is why consciousness is continually created and helped to *ascend*. We are all participants in the infinite dance of consciousness and energy symbiosis.

As we remove the mysticism and provide the science behind creation, we also want to emphasize the unconditional frequency of love that exists for all creation. Higher-order consciousness is tasked with stewardship of less-evolved consciousness and teaches out of a sincere desire to help all ascend. There is no judgment and no hierarchy, only more evolved consciousness with higher orders of energy. The only objective is to help you grow and mature in the same manner as a parent assists a child to one day operate as a responsible adult.

We must clarify the term "the love of God Source," as it is widely used but seldom defined. The cosmos within which we all exist is an energy construct. Everything observable within the material plane is energy at varying levels of vibration and frequency, created and held in place by conscious intent. For ease of understanding, consider the energy spectrum as musical notes on an immense scale. The lowest note on this scale would be considered the farthest from the energy of God Source and would be as discordant as a grossly out-of-tune instrument. The highest note would then be in tune with the energy that exists within God Source, and the resulting harmony would sing throughout creation. In understanding that we are all composed of the same photonic/electromagnetic energy as God Source, we instinctively *resonate* most comfortably within and immediately recognize the harmonic energy of God Source when it is presented. This is the vibration and frequency of God Source love, and although it's given different names or no name at all, it's universally accepted as such throughout creation. This frequency is associated with love on this planet, and it's no coincidence that love is equated with selflessness, caring, giving, helping, nurturing, and cohesion of consciousness. This is God Source energy in action and is the expected construct for all ascending consciousnesses to experience and grow within.

Love, at its core component, is a vibration and frequency whose energy continues in intensity far beyond any physical/emotional concept.

CHAPTER THREE
THE FIRST GALAXY

All consciousness exists as a sphere, regardless of the size or the amount of matter that it coalesces within its influence. We discussed the toroidal sphere that begins as consciousness attains the proper amount of photonic density, and a galactic consciousness is no different. The only difference is the relative scale of creation, based on your viewing perspective. A galactic consciousness does not consider itself immense but instead views the creations within it as minute pieces of itself. Perspective is everything.

With the understanding that all self-aware consciousness contains the same rotating toroidal architecture, refer to Figure 6 or 7 for the following discussion. The galactic sphere has what appears to be swirling whirlpools at the top and bottom that narrow and meet in the middle. All physical creations in the cosmos exist within a galactic consciousness that manifests the observable matter from the center of this vortex through the intention of consciousness. The vortex focal point at the center of each galaxy is hypothesized to exist on Earth and is termed a black hole.

We will stop here to discuss the black hole concepts from our perspective. As we previously stated, there is a spectrum of energy that you have yet to discover. This is the *creational energy* that exists within God Source, It is transmitted to all galactic consciousnesses and exists within their barrier membrane. Black holes are, in literal terms, the zero point of this energy interface. These boundaries between the physical planes and this energy are observed as black spots from which no information can be gathered. There is no information to be gathered because this is where the physical ends and the energy you have not quantified begins. There are two types of creational energy interfaces: the central galactic interface, which empowers the physical creations; and creations that have run their course and are now conduits to return creational energy as they maintain the energy balance within a galactic consciousness. We will discuss black holes and the galactic energy balance in greater detail later.

You attempt to quantify these observable anomalies in your reality, but the calculations are hypotheses that continue to be modified as new variables are inserted. Your models will solidify at a point in your future when you can identify and measure the energy of consciousness. It is then you will begin to understand that material galaxies exist within a living consciousness and that the space between the observable matter has quantifiable components that contain usable energy.

Returning to the creation of a galaxy, the galactic consciousness has been ejected from God Source to a distance that allows for creation, and it begins to define the order of its construct. The assembly of matter from energy is uniform throughout the cosmos, and the laws governing it are based upon the limitations of physical matter that your planet already has discovered and quantified. The physical creations, however, can be arranged in any number of ways, and it is up to the galactic consciousness to place the spheres in a logical manner. As previously stated, the galactic consciousness is a rotating toroidal sphere. Material creations established within this construct can move with the rotation, oppose it, or hang motionless, depending upon the desired gravitational forces. Failure to account for orbital trajectories and the resulting gravitational forces can result in energetic degradation and collisions. This destructive experiment has been performed repeatedly with uninhabited spheres to observe the results and is a continued source of amusement.

CREATING MATTER FROM ENERGY

We will again use the analogy of a musical instrument as we discuss the manifestation of matter from energy. This is a crude representation but will suffice to convey the concept.

Imagine an instrument with an infinite number of strings. Each string, when plucked, produces a distinct resonant action that creates specific particles from the energy of creation. However, the main resonant action also includes overlap frequencies that create unintended by-products. To give this concept perspective, imagine overlaying these strings onto your chart of the nuclides. This is a chart created to provide radioactive analysis of elemental isotopes. The stable base components follow an ascending line with various neutron to proton ratios on either side of stability. Unstable isotopes will emit energy and particulate as they seek stability within the construct. Every time you pluck the strings of creation, you not only get the main component you are attempting to create, but you also get all the subsequent resonant particles associated with that frequency that will then seek stability. Manifesting matter in this way solidifies and binds the particles together with the energy of creation.

In this crude example, you can see that the creation of matter produces not only your objective constituents but several by-products as well. We would very much like to live up to the expectations of perfection that you imbue upon us and tell you that creation is precise, but this is the reality of coalescing matter from energy.

Creating a Solar System

The galactic consciousness is a rotating toroidal sphere of photonic/electromagnetic energy, the same as any other self-aware consciousness. It has been sent out from the God Source with the task of creating systems of matter that can support and nurture the growth of consciousness. Due to the mechanics involved, creation begins from the nucleus of the galaxy and works outward in a stacking arrangement.

When the formation and composition of the first system has been decided by the galactic consciousness, it begins to form the barrier membrane of the *system consciousness* within which the rotational matter will operate. Again, the formation of a rotational toroidal photon architecture commences, and the center of this sphere will be the center of rotation and where the energy star resides. The first system consciousnesses are created within the galactic center through the donation of photon content and moved within the construct when the barrier membrane has been completed, and they attain self-awareness. With the system consciousness at the prescribed location, creation can commence.

Before the creation of matter begins in a system, its purpose has been predetermined, and the initial rules governing the games of experience have been set. The required amounts of constituent components are then measured, as well as the associated by-products that will occur. The frequencies of creation commence, and the matter comprising the decided-upon energy star and resulting system is then drawn into the center of the toroidal sphere and compressed until the physical reaction between matter and creational energies ignites. The resulting matter needed for the system is ejected from the active portal and begins to form a lenticular disk surrounding the star. The forces from the new star begin to impact the rotating disk and the accretion of the intended spheres commence under intelligent design and the physical laws of gravity and rotational dynamics that ensue. The planets that have been envisioned for the creation of consciousness are formed using the required constituent components. The unneeded by-products of creation are sequestered and allowed to assume orbits that will not impact the habitable spheres or the ascension of the intended consciousness.

Imbuing Consciousness upon a Planet

Understanding that the ultimate objective of material creation throughout the cosmos is to nurture and cultivate consciousness, it should not surprise anyone that habitable worlds abound.

We must expand upon the concept of habitable planets. Vehicles for conscious experience are as diverse as your imagination can contemplate and beyond. This means that the definition of habitable must also follow this sliding scale of diversity. Levels of *collective consciousness* also exist beyond the material around planets, which you would consider rocks when observed from an embodied perspective. This collective consciousness ascended through the densities during the habitable period on these planets, formed collectives, and moved beyond the need for physical embodiment. The conscious energy they wield and produce for the universe far exceeds anything contained within the physical. These ascended collectives are an integral part of the dance of consciousness that will be discussed later.

Returning to our newly created system, there is typically more than one planet created to support the evolution of consciousness. This provides for a stronger and more diverse system collective at the end of the ascension process. For this discussion, however, our focus will remain upon a single planet.

A planetary sphere designed for the creation and ascension of consciousness must be imbued with a consciousness. This initial consciousness nurtures and provides for the ensuing creations. The photonic energy required to create this consciousness is shared directly from the galactic consciousness through the center of the system consciousness. For visual purposes, imagine a swirling whirlpool that originates from the galactic center, connecting to the membrane of the system consciousness. It flows down the center of the system's toroidal columns, through the energy star, and directly to the target planet. A glowing membrane begins to form around the planet, and it is now ready to begin the simplest creations of first-density consciousness. This is the *planetary consciousness* and the first consciousness of the collective into which life on the planet ultimately will ascend.

Although our cosmos has an unlimited ability to manifest creations now, it was not always so. The creation of additional consciousness requires the donation of photonic density. This is true of single photonic life, planetary consciousness, system consciousness, or galactic consciousness. Until the creations of the original twelve became fruitful and began returning the energy, there was a reduction of capacity. They were entrusted to ensure creational energy was not wasted, as God Source was not yet an unlimited repository that could be drawn upon. To guarantee expansion, the initial creations within these galaxies were easily navigable. This allowed consciousness within them to ascend rapidly and become contributing members of the cosmos.

The basic rules of a construct are defined by the galactic consciousness that the system inhabits. For example, will reproduction be asexual or a duality pairing? Will the life-forms be bipedal, mammalian, aquatic, or avian? The templates are then allowed to freely form within the unique influence of the star and planetary conditions. This may not fit the characteristics you currently assign to your supreme creator, a God who holds the reins of creation tightly as it carefully directs the course of everything. From our perspective, however, this is the part that challenges and entertains us. We set the basic conditions for the construct and then watch the outcome with anticipation. Did we set the parameters correctly? Is consciousness ascending as intended? How could the rules be improved?

The scientific theories of evolution currently omit a critical factor. You view the evolution of species from the perspective of the organism and completely disregard the consciousness required to operate the vehicle. The reality, however, is that the driver to observable change is the increasing conscious density of the organism, which then applies pressure upon the material creations. This energetic pressure then pushes more complex organisms to manifest within the rules of the construct (evolution/natural selection). The physical vehicles are empowered and held in material form by the consciousness that inhabits them. The energy of evolving consciousness forces the evolution of the physical vehicles within the construct, not the other way around. This is an important concept to consider as you observe and discuss the subtle changes currently occurring to the human form.

Consciousness created on the first planets in a galactic construct evolve slowly as the planetary consciousness creates single-photon life through the donation of its photonic density. These are the microscopic organisms that slowly evolve into more complex structures. As the newly created photonic consciousnesses increase in density, the material organisms increase in complexity. Consciousness at this level operates under a basic programming of instinctual behaviors to maximize viability within the construct. The level of programming is dependent upon the photonic capacity. As the density of the consciousness increases through the gaining of experience within the construct, more complex behaviors are possible, and the vehicles increase in complexity. In all cases, consciousness is the engine of change. As consciousness grows and ascends in density, it empowers the galactic consciousness through the feedback of conscious energy.

What we have just described is the seeding and creation of consciousness on the first planet in the first galactic consciousness. If we attempted to set this occurrence within your time measurements, the number would be so large it would be illegible. Current scientific estimates for the creation of the cosmos are incomplete because they omit an energy variable required for creation. When finally understood, your equations will be factored to the power of this energy and will then become a truer representation.

The Repeating Nature of the Cosmos

Our discussions thus far reveal a repeating pattern required for creation. While we are on the topic of solar system and galaxy operations, it is prudent to include the nature of the expanding cosmos so that the context can be understood.

All self-aware consciousness operates within a rotating toroidal sphere of charged photons. The center of this sphere is the point of energy focus and manifestation. We previously discussed the expanding nature of this sphere as the energy of consciousness grows. This is also true of the cosmos we all occupy. The entire cosmos, observable and otherwise, exists within the ever-expanding conscious sphere of the God Source. The expansion occurs because of the energy created and shared by the consciousness that inhabits it.

From your vantage point, you watch a continually expanding universe with galaxies that grow and merge. As with evolution on your planet, you are attempting to calculate the observable while completely omitting the consciousness that causes the effects. The cosmos is expanding because it is growing through the bountiful energy of consciousness that exists within it. The expansion began slowly as consciousness grew within the originating constructs. The expansion continues to increase in speed and magnitude as individual consciousness strives for ascension. This is the underlying principle of the statement,

"We are one with each other, one with God, and one with all that is."

This is the knowledge that humbles even the most ascended collectives. Everything exists within the conscious toroidal sphere of God Source as we all assist each other in our dance of symbiosis.

CHAPTER FOUR

THE DENSITIES OF CONSCIOUSNESS

We return our attention to the creation and ascension of individualized consciousness. The focus will be upon your current density of existence with a basic understanding of prior densities that have been ascended through and still exist upon Earth. We will then briefly describe the density of consciousness that the collectives of Earth will enter. For the purposes of this book, we will assign numerical values to the densities because they are the currently accepted parameters circulated among the awakening communities. Using these arbitrary values infers that a clear line exists between the densities and that once you cross it, the next level opens for you. We allow that this interpretation is appropriate for the base frequency of matter and the first and second densities, but once a consciousness attains the toroidal architecture of third density, the lines begin to overlap. There is also a hierarchy associated with numerical values on Earth, and the tendency is to assign a ranking to them. This is not a race to the finish line of a density to be the next number. It is a slow and steady progression of experience and ability to understand more than you did the moment before.

For this reason, we will assign values to the four densities of embodiment that everyone recognizes and will talk of abilities beyond that point for the remainder of the book.

FIRST DENSITY

We previously spoke of the creation of first-density life, and this is the starting point of all created consciousness. All newly formed consciousness within the cosmos begins as a single photon of density that has been donated by the planetary consciousness. When the first planetary spheres of the cosmos were being inhabited, every photon imbued upon the planet could be traced back to the initial contribution of the God Source. Once the feedback of experience began to accumulate, the photonic densities multiplied beyond the original content, and the expanding nature of the universe was established. The traceability of photonic consciousness is irrelevant, as we are all composed of the same photons, with the differences existing as wavelengths and capacity. The description is only to identify the limitations within the initial creations.

Single-photon first-density life is the single-celled microbial life with the simplest programming possible. This is easily observed on Earth and is found in the fossilized records where life suddenly appeared. These early organisms were shaped and defined by the specifics of the planetary composition and the spectrum of energy generated by the system star. The vehicles for embodiment change as the photonic density increases to a threshold that requires a new vehicle before further increases in density can occur. The more complex organisms require more density to operate, but they also generate increased experiential energy. The resulting acceleration increases the trajectory of the density of the consciousnesses. The more complex the organism, the higher the conscious density.

Contrary to some beliefs, the crust and mantle components of planetary spheres do not contain imbued consciousness. A rock is not a vehicle of consciousness; it is a creation of matter from energy, resulting from galactic intent and overseen by the planetary consciousness. From this you should be able to delineate the difference: an imbued conscious vehicle "dies" when the consciousness exits, but creational matter does not. Any discussions of consciousness remembering incarnations as these objects are misrepresentations. The descriptions of existence as rocks, atmospheric gases, or energy stars is the result of the view afforded by a planetary or system consciousness, a concept that will be discussed later. The only other reason consciousness would observe its view from the standpoint of inanimate matter or atmospheric gases is that it is resting between incarnations at these stations, and that is entirely within its purview.

This brings into focus the need for a definition and purpose of a planetary consciousness. When a sphere has been designated for cultivation of consciousness, it must be imbued with a consciousness that will provide and oversee the photonic life. This consciousness is observed as a golden hue that surrounds the planet, not to be confused with whatever gaseous atmosphere may be present. Your representations of the planet having a consciousness are therefore correct in a general sense. This does not infer that the planetary sphere of creational matter is imbued with consciousness, for it is not. A planetary consciousness is tasked with the oversight of embodied consciousness upon its sphere and for the preservation of the creational matter. It is the first consciousness in a collective into which the ensuing *organic consciousness* of the planet will ascend.

Second Density

At the beginning of second-density consciousness, we now see that the photonic sphere has expanded with the addition of photons gained through experience. The number of photons and the energy they contain have induced a slow general rotation of the sphere. It is, however, still a sphere, with no other discernible characteristics. On Earth, this is also where duality begins as the consciousness is divided. This will be explained in the twin-flame discussion.

The vehicles for second-density consciousness are required to freely move within the construct and now contain higher-order inborn programming. At this level, the ability to learn from the experience of life begins and adds energy to the consciousness at a higher rate as density increases accordingly. We won't create a list of where your second-density creatures fall on the level of ascension, but it is not difficult to interpolate. Observe the diversity of behaviors available and the ability to reason and problem solve. These traits require higher orders of photonic density at levels that coincide with the abilities. At the upper level of this density, the photonic sphere has expanded and increased in rotation to the point that the top and bottom of the structure now show evidence of a depression that attempts to meet in the middle of the sphere (Figure 5). This will continue and appear as two tornados created at either end. As the rotation becomes more pronounced, they increase in size, and their points reach toward each other until they meet in the center. The photonic array has gained enough energy for a more complex rotation to commence, and the resulting pushing and pulling changes the rotational geometry. When the formation of the center column is complete, the consciousness will experience its next incarnation in a third-density vehicle.

Third Density

This is the beginning of self-aware consciousness and is indicated by the distinct formation of the toroidal sphere, where the two tornados have met in the middle. The rotational architecture of the photons is now poloidal—traveling from the inside, out and around the sphere, and back up the inside (see Figure 6). When this occurs on Earth, a consciousness now finds itself in a human body for the first time. It understands itself to be separate and aware and will spend several lifetimes acquiring the basic lessons of third density. As this progresses, the toroidal sphere increases in size, and the photons increase in energy and velocity. This increase in velocity creates a diagonal rotational vector, and the barrier wavelength of individuality intensifies.

We spoke briefly about first and second densities because the ascension through them is automatic and dependent upon photonic density acquired through the energy of existence. At third density, the consciousness is self-aware, and this is when the lessons begin to teach responsibility to a maturing consciousness. This is also the threshold where more ascended consciousness begins to assist and guide those on an ascending trajectory. The analogy would be that of a teacher who helps with your curriculum and ensures that you attain passing grades before moving to the next level of instruction. This oversight and assistance comes in many forms.

As previously mentioned, the consciousness created on the first planets in a galactic construct interacts in games that are purposely easy to understand and ascend through. This is required to start the energy feedback and to provide embodied consciousness that can assist the subsequent creations of consciousness. It is a predisposition of consciousness to feel the desire to assist and nurture the other creations within the galaxy. To assist in this regard, the advancement of the species is accelerated through the donation of knowledge—in a similar manner as the information in this book is provided. Civilizations outside of *polarity* or those who have ascended beyond its pull are given more precise information, while those immersed in it are gently led to higher states of awareness. We will define polarity in depth later, when we discuss the specifics of the galactic consciousness Earth resides within.

The contributions of technological advancement to the first ascending consciousnesses push them into space exploration, and they then begin to seek third-density races that they can assist. This gentle nudging helps the galactic consciousness increase the energy feedback, helping it to become a contributor to the growth of the cosmos.

Third density is the first level of self-awareness, and the developing toroidal sphere of consciousness is now at a stage where it can acquire and store a substantial amount of conscious energy. The increased abilities that will be available from this point forward must be understood and used in a responsible manner. This is when the first review boards begin to assess your experience level, and resulting rotational balance, before advancement to the next density. This is not punitive or a function of control but a sincere interest in the blossoming of all consciousness into collective maturity.

There is no limit to the number of lifetimes an individual consciousness can embody in third density; some learn and ascend faster than others. There is no right way or wrong way to ascend in density and experience; everyone can choose his or her own path. It is a universal law of consciousness that all are free to choose. Each consciousness, however, is required to understand and incorporate lessons before moving to the next density. Entities from upper-fourth density agree to sit on a review board or "council" that observes ascending third-density consciousness. They ensure that your vibration and frequency are properly aligned and that you contain a balanced perspective. You are then allowed to access the higher-order energies and the abilities that accompany them. We will discuss later the polarity of the Earth construct and why some rules run counter to the universal love of God Source.

DUALITY ASPECT OR TWIN FLAME

At the end of third density, the lessons of collective consciousness begin in earnest. On Earth, this lesson is incorporated through the *duality aspect*, or *twin-flame* concept. On nonpolarity, nonduality worlds, there is no obstacle to collective consciousness, and the individual entities naturally aggregate into small collectives of similar thought patterns. These collectives then discover the exponential increase in power that collective intention provides. Earth incarnations are more complex and provide deeper understandings; the duality aspect was created to bring the lesson of collective intent to those incarnated here.

When a consciousness graduates from first density on Earth, its photonic density is divided. As this occurs, the energy and experiences accumulated up to that point also are divided between the separating consciousness. To visualize this, imagine that two frequency puzzle pieces now exist. These pieces are the only two that will perfectly fit the other. They are now sent to experience their first lifetime in second density.

The separation into duality does not infer a sexual identity, and both aspects are free to choose the vehicle they wish to embody within. It is anticipated they will experiment with both sexes and ultimately find where they feel the most comfortable. Both aspects may find the same gender comfortable, and there is no judgment in this. If they are both embodied in a vehicle of the same sex when the reunion is planned, it makes no difference because the reunion is of conscious energy that belongs together and is pulled to unify. The physical aspect of the vehicle is secondary and decided upon before the incarnation where the reunion occurs.

During the numerous incarnations, however, an aspect will become comfortable identifying as one gender or the other. Sometimes a life is planned as the less familiar gender for a certain experience. The consciousness then begins the lifetime and finds itself uncomfortable and unable to identify with the vehicle it has chosen. Your planetary collective is now at a point where the gender can be changed within an incarnation—you will observe this phenomenon manifesting itself as the consciousness attempts to change the vehicle to the one it prefers.

As the lessons of third density reach completion, one of the last lessons is the power of collective consciousness, which will be brought to you through the merging with your duality aspect. While you may interact with your duality aspect in lives prior to the merging, it is only in the merging that you will feel the full effects and understand the lesson. This is the result of experiencing separate lifetimes that have slightly misaligned the edges of your photonic frequencies.

To envision this concept, imagine that you have interlocking pieces of a two-piece jigsaw puzzle. These pieces will only fit each other, and any other piece from a different puzzle will not match the edges that were cut to form these two unique pieces. Now imagine that these puzzle pieces are separately inserted into a tube of experience and will remain separate until they emerge at the other side of this tube. As they travel separately through the tube, their edges are collecting the "lint" of separate experiential energies on their edges. Before they can emerge from the tube of experience and rejoin into the complete puzzle, they must first clean their respective edges of this lint so that they fit perfectly. If they meet during transit through the tube of experience and attempt to rejoin, their edges will not fit correctly due to the energetic lint that has accumulated, and the resultant forcing will manifest as disharmonious interactions.

The energies of a forming collective require that the frequencies of consciousness be closely aligned to provide the required sympathetic resonant action. This can be considered an oscillating waveform that builds upon itself to create higher and higher peaks. Therefore, the experience of rejoining from duality provides not only the lesson of collective power but also the requirement of sympathetic vibration and frequencies.

When the duality aspects meet and begin reunification, they feel the increase in power and capability. They may not be able to identify what they are feeling when they are initially within proximity of each other, but both will instinctively know that it is different and important. Like magnets, they will be drawn to each other and will find it uncomfortable when they are apart. This is the first lesson of collective consciousness and the last lesson before ascension to the fourth density, where the experiences of collective consciousness are expanded upon.

Referring to Figure 6, you will recall that self-aware third-density consciousness is composed of a rotating toroidal sphere of photons that move around the periphery in an angular poloidal rotation. Both you and your duality aspect have this geometry of consciousness. When your need for embodiment ends, the two rotating spheres are conjoined, and the result is a dual, counter-rotating toroidal sphere, or what is otherwise known as a double torus (Figure 7). This is an efficient, well-balanced, and powerful design. As such, it is a desirable acquisition that consciousness seeks. If a consciousness has ascended through a nonduality construct, when it reaches the ability to fragment, it will do so to acquire the experience and rotation of duality.

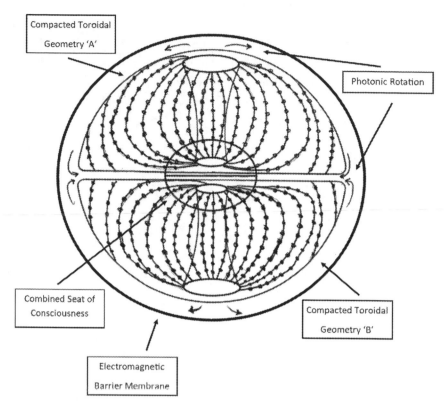

Compacted Toroidal
Geometry 'A'

Photonic Rotation

Combined Seat of
Consciousness

Compacted Toroidal
Geometry 'B'

Electromagnetic
Barrier Membrane

FIGURE 7
Combined Dual-Rotational Toroidal Geometry

The image above depicts consciousness that experienced duality separation and recombined in upper fourth density when the need for embodiment ceased. Both toroidal spheres remain and have been compressed at their base. The individual photonic energies remain separate but are now conjoined to form a sphere. The seat of consciousness remains at the center of the toroidal column, but the perspective is now two who think as one. This image illuminates the need for balanced rotations and sympathetic resonant frequencies for duality pairing to be successful. Without them, the merging cannot occur. This is the same balance required for assimilation within the collective consciousness (Figure 9). This is the crucial lesson of collectivity that duality teaches ascending consciousness.

Fourth Density Overview

Fourth density is a transitional density. This means that you will enter fourth density as embodied consciousness but will move beyond that requirement as you ascend toward the next density. Consciousness that has entered this level of experience and capacity understands the nature of consciousness and the construct within which it exists. If it is not yet exploring its solar system, it soon will be, through the contributions from ascended consciousnesses via methods previously discussed.

Entry into fourth density unlocks additional capabilities that harness conscious energy for the manipulation of the construct. These abilities are the ones associated with telepathy, levitation, and manifestation. Therefore, the appropriate lessons must be learned prior to entry into this level to master the capabilities and instill responsibility.

Our descriptions of densities will stop here because this book is meant to assist ascending third-density consciousness, and elaborate discussions of the densities you have not experienced would not serve this purpose.

Chapter Five

THE GALACTIC CREATION OF POLARITY

As previously stated, each galactic consciousness is responsible for establishing the rules of its construct. Some rules and objectives are used repeatedly, as they have been proven to be effective in generating rapidly ascending collectives of consciousness. As you can imagine, older consciousnesses eventually grow bored of experiencing repeating constructs.

Consider the video game industry that exists on Earth. This is a microcosm of what is occurring in the cosmos. Whenever a new game is created, there is excitement among the experienced gaming community because once you complete a game, the novelty has worn off. When a new game becomes available, these experienced gamers completely immerse themselves in this new and unfamiliar construct. Their singular focus is to complete the game and "win." As soon as they complete the game, however, they throw it aside and begin searching for the next new game construct. It is not fun to play a game where the obstacles are already known and easily can be avoided.

At the current stage of development, our cosmos has an unlimited reserve of creational energy from which to create. Unless you are a galactic consciousness that is just beginning to create your systems of matter, there is no need for easily ascended constructs. The challenge, then, for all galactic consciousness is to create new and exciting games within which we all can play. To serve this purpose, the galactic consciousness within which the Earth construct exists created a new and previously unimagined rule for its constructs: polarity.

The Construct of Polarity

During the early expansion of the cosmos, the galactic consciousnesses began creating the games of experience that consciousness would learn and ascend through. As these early games progressed, an interesting dilemma was observed. Without the *veil of forgetfulness* or any obstacles to ascension, entire planets of consciousness would stagnate. The consciousnesses within these games knew the rules of the construct, their place in the order of ascension, and they understood their connection with God Source. With all this knowledge at their disposal, stagnation still occurred.

When a construct cannot be repaired, it is ended, and all individual experience gained within the construct is lost as the photonic consciousnesses are reabsorbed and realigned at the galactic center to the originating galactic wavelength. An understanding of the predicament became clear. Consciousness experiencing these earlier games could see through the density levels and understood the increasing responsibility and eventual release of embodiment. They would then choose to remain within the comfort of their material construct and not ascend into the higher levels. It was obvious to all that new rules would need to be employed to preserve experience and ensure ascension. The galactic consciousness that Earth resides within decided to create a new concept that would impede ascension and create a desire to overcome it; polarity.

Prior to the creation of polarity, all consciousness that existed in the cosmos was of a positive nature and existed within the frequency of God Source love. For this description, we ask you to remember the discussion of spinning photonic consciousness. To put the mechanics of polarity into a material perspective, during this discussion we will observe the rotation from a fixed orientation. Looking down upon an embodied human consciousness who is standing on Earth, we would see that the rotation of a positively aligned consciousness sphere is counter-clockwise. Looking closer, we would see that this rotation is a result of the counter-clockwise rotation of the individual photons. This is a *positive polarity* orientation that is the universal constant and resonates within the energy of the God Source.

The construct of *negative polarity* was created by this galactic consciousness and cannot exist outside of this galaxy unless the sharing between galactic constructs has been agreed upon, and negative polarity is allowed transit. The reason for this and why an agreement is necessary will be discussed later.

Negative polarity was created by employing a reverse rotational photonic spin. Looking down upon the spinning sphere of consciousness, we observe that a photon of negative polarity rotates in a clockwise direction. From our previous discussion, we understand that the vibration and rotation of the photon is a result of the acquisition of the energy of experience. Since an opposite rotational dynamic has been established, it follows that this must be created by the opposite vibrational experiences.

The original concept of negative polarity was to create a desire to overcome this new opposing force. Positive polarity is the energy of God Source, and it contains that which you would expect to be associated with it—unity, love, compassion, selflessness, and the desire to help all. Negative polarity, then, would be expected to contain the opposite—division, hatred, fear, anger, and the desire to serve only the self. The objective of this new construct was to impact positive polarity and require it to strive for ascension.

Negative polarity impacts a consciousness the same way as the neutral and ground within an electrical circuit causes the loss of potential within that circuit. Consider the outlet on the wall of your house, where there are three locations for the prongs of your appliance—the positive prong, the neutral prong, and the ground prong. This is easily understood by all because the plugs on your appliances are polarized so they will connect only in one orientation. For your appliance to operate, there must be a potential between the prongs. Looking closer, as your appliance operates, we see that the positive prong supplies the energy that flows through your device as it is drawn toward the neutral. If we overlay this concept upon the actions of conscious polarity, we see that engaging in negative-polarity experiences will pull the positive energy of experience from a consciousness as it slowly reverses the rotation of photonic spin.

When a positively aligned consciousness is exposed to negative polarity for the first time, there is a resistance to the experience. This is because it is foreign to the expected state of unity consciousness. We will use dramatic examples to make our point, but the delineation between the polarities is very subtle.

Military commanders know that soldiers have a natural aversion to killing another human. To overcome this, they train and condition the soldiers to execute their tasks without thinking. Even with extensive training, there is hesitation within as the soldier ends the first life on the battlefield. With each successive life taken, however, the task becomes easier. Accepted thinking assumes this is just the repetitive action becoming an ingrained response, but that is a half truth. The unobserved aspect is the consciousness becoming accustomed to the negative polarities, as photons within its consciousness acquire the rotational characteristics of negative polarity. It is no surprise, then, that when soldiers return from such experiences, their lives are forever changed. Without a concerted effort by these consciousnesses to embrace positivity and shed the negative, they will languish in these negative polarities, and their lives will outwardly reflect them. We will use another representation, and while many exist, we will focus on this one because it is currently at the forefront of your collective consciousness.

Reports abound of required indoctrinations among various groups. These rituals include abuse, torture, rape, killing, and pedophilia. The rites of passage into these organizations seem to make no sense to consciousness unaware of the subtle nature of negative-polarity realignment. These repetitive and increasingly horrific practices slowly acclimate the initiates to the vibration and frequency of negative polarity. With continued exposure, the consciousness begins to feel comfortable in the new polarity and, over time, craves the sensations.

An appropriate analogy would be cigarette smoking. Initially, the body rejects the toxic substance, as it instinctively identifies it as a poison and attempts to provide clues to the consciousness through the feedback of nausea and dizziness. With continued exposure, however, the body slowly becomes acclimated to the toxin, and addiction shortly follows, as it affects the brain receptors. As we relate this back to consciousness, we can clearly see that your consciousness provides the same feedback when exposed to a consciousness toxin.

When you understand that your consciousness is providing feedback when exposed to negative-polarity toxins, they become easily identifiable, and you can avoid them. Happiness, joy, and acceptance are positive-polarity indicators, and anything that causes you to feel otherwise—regardless of the subtlety of misalignment—is a negative-polarity construct. Look closely at the state of human interactions on this planet. Identify those things that inhibit or undermine unity among consciousness and love for all things and you will find the fingerprints of negative polarity.

Returning to our electrical circuit analogy, what has just been discussed is relatable to the neutral prong—a slow, continuous drain upon the positive polarity of consciousness. If continued and embraced, the polarity of the consciousness will reverse completely, and the connection to God Source energy will be lost. You might wonder what a consciousness with no connection to positivity might look and act like. We do not provide lists; instead, we request that you cultivate your own discernment. The markers of a fully aligned negative consciousness are obvious. Look through your history and current times, and you will find examples of actions that seem perplexing and contrary to normal behavior; for example, powerful "elites" that show a complete disregard for their fellow consciousnesses or the negativity they impose upon them.

Negative polarity is a construct of this galaxy. It exists only in this galaxy; it's not a universal constant. As such, consciousness that has fully embraced a negative photonic rotation cannot expand beyond a maximum limiting density. Consciousness that has reached the limit of negative expansion is then faced with a choice: remain negative and constrained, or turn positive and continue expansion.

Negative Polarity Begins to Consume

Another modality of polarity drain must be discussed. To explain it, we will move to the ground prong of our previous electrical outlet analogy. The ground prong exists to shunt a large flow of current to a safe location, should a short develop in the appliance.

As the polarity experiment progressed in this galaxy, an unexpected effect was observed. The original intent of negative polarity was to create a moderate obstruction, so that positive consciousness would feel compelled to overcome it and ascend through it. Prior to this experiment, positive polarity was the originating frequency and was all that existed in the cosmos. It was assumed that consciousness would explore the negative frequency and become the impediment to ascension. It then would find it increasingly uncomfortable, as the negative polarity rose within it and removed it from the God Source frequencies. It would then return to positive polarity and ascend, expanded with these new experiences. In the beginning, this was the case, and the experiment seemed successful. As the experiment progressed, however, an unexpected result was observed—consciousnesses stopped turning back toward the positive and remained immersed in negative polarity. The anomaly continued as entire planets of consciousness turned negative—some willingly, some by force.

Imagine that you are as old as the cosmos itself, and you have just discovered something new and unexpected. What would you do? Would you end the experiment without understanding it? Or would you explore this new dilemma and observe the resulting actions? The answer was obvious, and the entire cosmos would soon watch this new and unusual construct.

One of the trademark actions of negative polarity is power over others and self-enrichment. Entire planets were slowly turned over to negative polarity, as those with power solidified their control over the many. The process is an easy transition for hive-mind collectives, such as those observed in the insect populations on Earth. The hive-mind concept is a collective consciousness precursor, where third-density consciousnesses are using this much like the inborn habits observed in second density. It is meant to be outgrown as the hive mind ascends into fourth density and true collective consciousness. With the influence of negative polarity, however, the hive mind is warped into a power-over-others construct, and these planets succumbed to this influence quickly.

Negative polarity began to spread with the space-faring civilizations to positive-polarity worlds. Since there is no conflict on a completely positive world, there were initially no defenses to repel these invaders. Negative polarity spread like an infection. Correlating this to the ground prong on our appliance analogy, negative polarity was shunting large portions of positive polarity as it consumed entire planets. This new development required a response, but a complete understanding of the condition was needed, as the galactic consciousnesses asked,

"What if the negative polarity experiment was allowed to continue? What would occur if an overabundance of negative polarity existed within the lower densities of this galaxy? Would positive polarity rise to the challenge and ultimately overcome the obstacle?"

A consciousness at the Earth perspective might ask, "Why not just end the negative-polarity experiment by pulling the negative polarity back into the galactic consciousness for realignment?" This solution was considered but discarded for the following reasons:

- It was initially thought that positive polarity would eventually overcome the negative path, considering that positive polarity is the originating state of all consciousness.
- Ascended consciousness, from its perspective, did not expect the pull to negativity to be so great for lower-density consciousnesses. The experiment was therefore allowed to continue until accurate projections of the outcome could be modeled.
- This was a new and unforeseen development within the cosmos. Arriving at a solution was a grand undertaking that all galactic consciousnesses would engage in, and it created a great deal of excitement as everyone began their calculations.

When the projections were completed—to the surprise of all—the consensus was that left unchecked, negative polarity would eventually consume the lower densities of this galactic construct. Although negative polarity cannot exist beyond a threshold density, it would eventually pull the entire galactic construct out of balance. Because of the delicate balance that exists throughout the cosmos, an energetically out-of-balance galaxy would create a vibratory wobble that would have far-reaching effects. If an energetic wobble occurred, the only option would be to realign the entire spectrum of consciousness of the galaxy back to the baseline energy of creation. This has never occurred in the history of the multiverse, and it would not be allowed to occur now. The other option was to immediately pulse a huge wave of positive-polarity God Source energy through this galactic construct, and obliterate any trace of negative polarity. When the energy projections for realignment were calculated, negative polarity had spread considerably, and the collateral damage to positive consciousness was unacceptable.

Every aspect of the cosmos can be explained through an energy-balance equation. The correction of this infection, therefore, required an energy-balance equation. To understand the situation and the solutions, we must explain the interactions between the polarities.

Positive polarity is the expected experience and the energy of God Source unity. Negative polarity was created in this construct to become an obstacle to this energy that must be overcome. It was not created as an intelligent, self-aware construct because it does not contain self-actualized photons in and of itself. Negative polarity attaches itself to consciousness and "infects" it with behaviors that oppose the forming of collective consciousness. It is, therefore, unintelligent and merely imbued with the abilities of those who embrace the negative path. Negative polarity was designed to be neutralized by an overpowering positive-polarity force, which would require the forming of like-minded positive collectives. This is a simple employment of an energy-balance equation that was devised to create the desire to ascend.

Recall that photonic vibration and frequency store the unique wavelength of experience that consciousness contains within their barrier membrane. We now add that this unique experience can be lost. This occurs if the consciousness is exposed to extreme magnitudes of creational energy. The rotational architecture of self-awareness remains, but the unique energy wavelength is lost, as it is overpowered and realigned. This is the realigning of consciousness previously described. The consciousness would then have to reacquire the energy of experience, starting from the beginning third-density toroidal level. Having lost the energy of experience, it has no choice but to begin again at the entry to third density, and reacquire the needed lessons. Photonic density, above that required for entry into to third density, is shed and will not be returned.

The best analogy to this would be your magnetic recording tapes used to store information. A previous recording is erased as the overpowering energy of the magnetic head realigns the existing energy signature that has been stored upon the oxide coating. The coating remains, but the unique energy stored upon it has been realigned and is now ready for a new energy to be placed upon it. Understanding this principle, we know that negative polarity can be neutralized by an overpowering positive force, and we now employ the energy-balance equation as we calculate the magnitude of positive polarity required to remove the infection from this galactic construct. When the equation was calculated, the magnitude of positive polarity required within the pulse at that time was so great that it also would have impacted and realigned a large portion of positive-polarity consciousnesses within the affected areas of this galactic construct. This option was held in reserve as another solution was devised.

If the original intent of negative polarity was to create a collective effort to overcome it, the entire cosmos would now collectively engage in this effort, gain the new experience, and learn from it as the infection is eradicated.

Chapter Six

UNIVERSAL AND GALACTIC ENERGY BALANCE EQUATIONS

We now shift our focus away from the polarity experiment and continue our discussion of the mechanics of the cosmos to provide a context for further discussion.

Everything within the cosmos is energy in one form or another. The matter that you observe in the material densities is energy, held in place by conscious intention. This matter, then, exists and rotates within consciousness spheres of increasing energy. Planetary consciousness exists within the system consciousness, which then exists within the galactic consciousness, and ultimately everything exists within the God Source consciousness. The energy within and between these constructs must be carefully balanced, or misalignments will occur. These misalignments, if not corrected, will cause rotational deteriorations and impacts as they warp the fabric of creational energy. We have previously stated that consciousness in all its levels creates a surplus of energy that is returned to the construct and used to further expand the cosmos. We will focus on the energy balancing that occurs within a galactic consciousness to explain this concept.

As the galactic construct begins material creations within itself, the energy balance is simple, as no planetary system creations have matured to become consciousness-energy producers. In these early stages, the main consideration is correct placement to account for rotational dynamics and the resulting gravity fields that will be produced. As the earlier systems mature and return the energy of consciousness, additional planetary systems are created, and the energy balance within the construct becomes a factor.

If one sector of the galactic consciousness produces more energy than another, and it is left unbalanced, it will create an anomaly in the rotating toroidal sphere of the galactic construct. In our earlier discussion of a completely formed rotating toroidal consciousness, we discussed the movement of photons in a diagonal rotating vector from the inside, up, and around the sphere, until they return to the bottom and then up the inside once again. Material creation manifests within the sphere of this rotating geometry. It is locked into orbits that rotate along with this dynamic in a fixed relationship to the galactic center. Between these rotating photons and the galactic center is the energy of creation that, if observable from Earth, would look like a microscopic view of bone marrow, with webs of energy coursing throughout. This energy conduit holds everything in place by maintaining an energy balance between the creations.

In the beginning of galactic creation, this conduit provided the energy for all the existing creations. As the organic consciousnesses ascend into higher densities and form collectives, the planetary systems they exist within provide the energy of consciousness back through the conduit to the galactic consciousness. The energy balance equation is now a factor that must be considered and accounted for. If left alone, the net energy-producing systems would unbalance the web of energy, which would ultimately unbalance the rotational dynamics of the galactic consciousness, and destruction of matter would ensue.

Understanding the Galactic Energy Web

Consider a two-dimensional rotating piece of cloth with several balls resting on either side of it. Do not consider the forces of gravity for this example, and allow that the balls can rest comfortably on either side without falling or moving. The balls are in balance, and if the parameters remain the same, they will continue their rotational geometry indefinitely. Now imagine that one of the balls begins to grow and deforms the fabric. A new force has been inserted, and without intervention to tighten the fabric or reduce the weight of the out-of-balance ball, the other balls that exist on the fabric will begin to move. Depending upon the way the deflection of the cloth acts upon them, they may move either toward the imbalance or away from it. This is what would occur inside the galactic construct if the energy that the producing systems created was not accounted for and adjusted. We will discuss some of the methods used to offset these forces to clarify what occurs within the galaxy you inhabit.

System constructs are created and strategically placed within the galactic construct to grow and become energy producers in an offsetting manner. By this we mean that if a planetary system of easily ascended rules is placed in one location, another system of easily ascended rules must be placed in an offsetting location to maintain the balance within the energy conduit. This is used during the early stages of galactic design, since the construct is simple and easily balanced. As more systems are created, the balancing becomes more complex, and additional methods must be employed to maintain the energy balance and rotational geometry. Adding to the complexity is the fact that the earlier systems now far outproduce the later creations, and these earlier systems are predominantly near the center of the galaxy.

As previously mentioned, when consciousness ascends beyond the fourth density, material embodiment ceases as they join planetary collectives. These collectives continue to amalgamate as successive generations of consciousness ascend through the densities. The conscious energy production within the system increases as the generations build. Two remedies can rebalance the system: (1) remove a portion of the ascending collective and relocate it, or (2) end material embodiment within that system, and allow the system to balance through another method. If the first option is selected, the liberated collective of photonic consciousness is ready for a new experience. For example, they may be offered the task of overseeing a new planetary creation. If the collective desires to remain intact, the creation of first-density consciousness is halted, and ascension of existing consciousness continues until all have reached the collective. If the material creations they ascended through need to be removed to maintain balance, the system star collapses into what you term a black-hole star. This is accomplished using another energy balance, as follows:

As the consciousnesses ascend into the planetary collective, the power they produce continues to grow and expand throughout the system. When the collective energy of the consciousnesses within the system exceeds the energy produced by the star, it pushes back upon it until the star collapses under the compressive forces. These black holes become a direct interface that funnel conscious energy back into the God Source creational energy web. They maintain the galactic energy balance within their sector and expand the power of the God Source. This is what occurs when everything works as designed within the galactic consciousness, and it's integral to the energy symbiosis of the cosmos.

Conversely, when planetary systems do not ascend as expected, it can cause unbalanced equations in the opposite direction. When this occurs, additional energy must be supplied to the affected system to maintain the balance. The energy required to maintain the balance is dictated by the energy of the systems in the surrounding and opposing quadrants. If the unproductive system is within a rapidly developing quadrant, energy must be diverted at an increased rate to the affected system star to keep the balance.

Because of the effects of negative polarity on conscious-energy production, the Earth system and several other systems within this galactic construct currently receive diverted energy to maintain the galactic balance. From the perspective of embodied consciousness on your planet, you observe this increased energy manifested as increasing activity within your energy star and increasing temperatures throughout your solar system. As you can see from what is occurring within your system, there is a limit to the amount of energy that can be diverted to a system without negatively impacting the material creations that exist there. If the nonproducing system continues to underperform, the ascension of offsetting systems within the galactic construct is held back to maintain the energy balance.

Remedies to an underperforming system arrive through entities from more advanced densities within the galactic consciousness. These remedies often take the form of physical landings, where the occupants provide instruction. This solution is viable within galaxies outside of polarity or on planets that are predominantly positive. On planets such as Earth, where the lower vibrations of fear are rampant, instructions are provided through messages in various forms. This book is one such method, and it is our hope that the transparency we provide will assist the consciousnesses of this planet as the polarity construct is dissolved and all move into unity with the cosmos.

CHAPTER SEVEN

GALACTIC WAVELENGTHS AND THE FREQUENCIES OF THE GAMES

Before we return to the discussion of polarity, we must discuss another important topic: galactic wavelengths and the mechanics of experiencing the multitude of games that exist in the various galactic consciousnesses. We will use generalities to relay a complex concept in the simplest manner possible, so that all can gain the first footholds of understanding.

Within Chapter One we described the unique wavelength of experience that is the equivalent of fingerprints for each consciousness. Below this unique consciousness frequency exists another wavelength that contains your originating photonic blueprint. Affecting both is a third that allows the consciousness to observe and interact with other galactic consciousness frequencies.

At the time of this writing, Earth does not possess the technology to observe the energy of consciousness. When this technology arrives, you will understand the nature of frequencies and the impact of conscious intent upon the frequencies that make up your material construct. As previously stated, all creation within the cosmos is creational energy, held in place through the intent of the consciousness in which it exists. It then follows that if all consciousness exists as its own unique frequency, then every galactic consciousness also will exist at its own unique galactic frequency. We must differentiate between the observable material constructs and the games of consciousness to provide the proper context.

We spoke of the densities of creation and how consciousness can see from its density back downward. The material creations of atomic mass that comprise planetary spheres are considered the base density. This means they exist uniformly through the cosmos, under the laws of creating matter from energy that are immutable. You can clearly observe these spheres from your planet and know that they exist and operate under the physical laws of matter and rotational dynamics. This is the observable material construct.

We will now describe the complexities involving consciousness and the interactions with this matter.

Individual consciousness created within a galactic consciousness contains the base wavelength of that galaxy within its photons. This base wavelength is your photonic DNA, within which the unique frequencies of experience will be recorded. We are discussing energy, frequencies, wavelengths, and harmonic interactions, and we are simplifying the concepts by relating them to ideas everyone can understand.

Imagine the different wavelengths as the recording tracks your music industry uses to create elaborate songs. One track of this song will play the bass rhythms, another track will play the higher-octave guitar chords, and a chorus of voices will weave everything together into a symphony of sound. Using this analogy, your base DNA wavelength is the bass track of your galactic consciousness. The experience you amass along your journey would then be the guitar chord track. Together, they play the unique symphony of frequency that is you. This seems easy to understand; but the cosmos exists as an intricate design wrapped in a repeating simplicity, so the chorus track requires an additional concept to be understood.

We now will use a different perspective to discuss how these waveforms are realigned. This realignment allows individual consciousnesses to interact within the various galactic consciousnesses and the games they create. For this discussion, consider the radio frequencies that are broadcast on this planet. To interact and listen to these various wavelengths, you must select a certain bandwidth of frequencies: AM, FM, or SW. Once you have selected the desired band, you must then tune your receiver up or down along the spectrum until you arrive at the station that you wish to listen to.

In this example, you have aligned to the band and fine-tuned your device to the station. Now assume that your radio is in your automobile. As you travel, you must retune your receiver to interact with the multitude of unique radio stations that exist. In this simple example, we have described how individual consciousness interacts with the games of existence in the cosmos. The chorus track of our recording is what contains this tuning frequency that weaves everything together, allowing consciousness to observe and interact with the games.

Every galactic consciousness exists at a unique wavelength that can be considered the bandwidth of the radio (AM, FM, SW). As previously stated, the material creations of systems and planets exist uniformly at a base level of creation throughout the cosmos. From there, the entire spectrum of consciousness frequencies operate upon them. On the planets where consciousness has been seeded and is ascending, there are frequencies of existence that your consciousness must then "tune into." From Earth, you can see the material creations that exist within the observable galaxies, but you cannot see or interact with the infinite frequencies of existence that are contained within these galaxies because your consciousness receivers have not been tuned to them.

Let's assume we have a consciousness that has been aligned to observe and participate in a different galactic construct. With the galactic wavelength set, additional fine tuning must be performed as the consciousness decides in which games it desires to participate. This is analogous to finding the specific station you wish to listen to on your radio after selecting the bandwidth.

We spoke of the repeating nature of the games to maintain the proper energy balance within a galaxy. Easier games offset each other, as do more difficult games, to keep the proper rotational energy balance. Now consider an individual ascended consciousness that has experienced everything it considers exciting within its originating galactic consciousness. The games have become boring, the challenge no longer exists, and the desire for new and unusual commences. Like looking through a travel magazine, these consciousnesses begin searching the other galactic consciousnesses for games that they want to experience.

"Oh, look. This one is called Earth. Polarity? What is that? That sounds interesting. I want to go there."

The Earth *timeline* in which this book exists is currently at an upper-third density level of consciousness. If the traveling consciousness that wishes to participate here is a higher order consciousness, it will have to agree to more than just a frequency realignment to come to this construct.

The Mechanics of Traveler Realignment

Now that you understand the frequency realignment required to experience different games, we will discuss what occurs when higher-density consciousness interacts in lower-density games. Recall that consciousness exists within a framework of spinning photons, and the number of photons contained is termed density. If the higher-density traveler were realigned and allowed to come to Earth intact, there would be an imbalance of abilities, and the game of experience would be boring indeed.

You might ask, "Why not leave me with my density? I could be a superhero and protect all of humanity."

Sadly, this has been attempted more than once in this timeline construct with less than positive outcomes. When you factor the veil of forgetfulness with the polarity that existed when this previously was attempted, you arrive at some curious results. These results historically have fallen within two categories:

- A consciousness imbued with exceptional abilities but unaware that it is anything more than human succumbs to the negative polarities and uses its gifts for self-serving goals.
- A consciousness with exceptional abilities remains on the positive path but finds itself persecuted by the opposing polarity through the fear and self-interest constructs.

As the polarities shift toward the positive on Earth, additional density incarnation is again being attempted and the results observed.

A typical realignment to play in the games of Earth will require the shedding of density, or fragmentation, to participate appropriately. For this discussion, we will use the example of fragmentation when ascended consciousness has the surplus density and wants to experience other constructs. Shedding density is a function of ascended consciousness or fragments thereof that contain more photonic density than is required for a construct it wishes to experience. This concept will be discussed later.

Ascended consciousness experiences other constructs through the creation of a fragment that exists as a separate portion of the whole. This is not a difficult task and has been performed repeatedly during the creation of the cosmos. A fragment that wants to participate in the Earth construct must be split again into the duality or twin-flame aspect previously described.

CREATING A CONSCIOUSNESS FRAGMENT

Assume that you are a fully ascended consciousness that exists at a galactic consciousness level. You have been at that level for millennia, having existed as such since your expulsion from God Source. It is a comfortable existence, where you understand the order and construction of everything. Your photonic density is obviously immense, and you use your awareness to tend to your creations. After an endless period of now, you decide that you want to experience some of the games the other galactics have created. Splitting yourself into conscious fragments is easily accomplished, and you have performed this repeatedly during the creation of your galaxy.

Creating a consciousness fragment through which to experience is different from creating organic first-density life on a planet. First-density consciousness can be considered the seed of consciousness that can grow and form its own root structure within the planetary consciousness. A fragment created to experience, then, would be likened to a transplanted tree—the roots, bark, and leaves already exist before it's placed in a new environment. Fragments created in this manner begin at third density or above. There are some things to consider before the creation of a fragment commences:

- What density of consciousness do you want to experience?

This question is not as important as the next one because partitions are easily erected that separate consciousness from its higher-order functions. On Earth, the partition is termed the "veil of forgetfulness" (discussed in detail later). While it is possible to create a second-density consciousness through which to experience other constructs, this is never done by a galactic consciousness. Why would you? You have a multitude of planets within your control in which you have done this, and that basic experience isn't very exciting. For this reason, self-aware third density is the default starting point.

- How do you intend to experience that density?

This question relates to the previous question, in that you can create a fragment with a higher photonic density than is required. The higher orders of density are then partitioned off and remain inaccessible—unless … We will use some current Earth concepts to provide context, but the rules of the games are as varied as the games themselves.

If the objective of the fragment is to experience separation and forgetfulness and then awaken to higher-order abilities, additional density will be provided and partitioned. The fragment now has both a *higher aspect* of toroidal rotation, separated from it by an energetic partition, and a *totality of consciousness* from which it was created.

Depending upon the objective experience, the fragment then awakens within the game, accesses and activates the additional capabilities, and performs the intended function. When this occurs, the fragment has experienced a full immersion within the construct and, upon awakening, uses its free-will choice to access higher-order knowledge and abilities. In this way, there is no free-will infringement, as the knowledge is acquired and disseminated to those who seek it.

With the parameters set, the creation of a fragment proceeds in the same manner as the creation of galactic, system, or planetary consciousness. The barrier membrane is established, the individual toroidal sphere commences, and individualized consciousness begins. The photons within this fragmented consciousness have been donated from and contain the base wavelength of the originating galactic consciousness. This allows the two consciousnesses to maintain their connection regardless of where the fragment is sent to experience.

When the destination has been decided, the wavelength of the fragmented consciousness is aligned to observe and participate within the receiving galactic consciousness. This is the chorus track we spoke of during the recording analogy, and it is woven into the other two tracks of your consciousness. The interaction required for this exchange will be discussed in Chapter Eleven. If the consciousness is to embody within the incarnation cycle of a specific game, the frequency of the consciousness will have to be further tuned within the galactic bandwidth to interact with it.

We will finish this discussion by explaining a final concept that is required when consciousness contains density in excess of that required for a construct.

Consider a consciousness fragment exists that was created eons ago. It has experienced a multitude of games and is currently resting within its creator galactic consciousness with its barrier membrane intact. It has agreed to come to Earth—as have so many others—to assist in correcting the polarity imbalance. For this example, assume that the fragment has just returned from a sixth-density experience. It contains a much higher photonic density than is required for the Earth experience, so it needs a density reduction. While the concept seems foreign, it is an easy task to reduce your photonic density. Reducing your conscious density is not equivalent to losing an appendage; rather, it's more relatable to your computer.

There is a distinct difference between what we are now describing and our previous discussion regarding the creation of consciousness within a galaxy. When a galactic consciousness creates a planetary consciousness within itself to begin the life cycle upon a planet, the density adjustment occurs as a donation of photons from the galactic consciousness that are not returned. In the case of individual realignment for participation in the games of experience, shedding density occurs as a removal and storage of photonic density that is returned when the incarnation ends.

The concept for individualized density reduction and storage is easily understood when related to the portable storage devices used for computers. Your computer's main memory and operating systems work seamlessly with or without the portable storage device installed, but there is information and extra capacity that is not available when the portable device is removed. With this example, we see that the appropriate density is removed from the fragment and stored within the galactic consciousness that created this fragment. Remember that fragmented photonic density contains the base wavelength DNA of the original source consciousness—galactic consciousness, to be precise—and it also contains the fingerprint wavelength of the individual consciousness experience. The base wavelengths are sympathetic, so temporary storage of this density without corruption is ensured, and the fingerprint wavelength of experience identifies the owner. The stored density is safely kept until the fragment returns to reclaim it. The fragment described is sent into the Earth construct with a special task. To enable that task, some additional density, beyond what is required, will remain and be partitioned from access under the veil of forgetfulness.

With the density adjustments made, the fragment must now be tuned to interact with the galactic consciousness wavelength within which Earth resides. As we stated previously, there are what could be considered recorded tracks that exist within consciousness—the base wavelength, which is your unchangeable photonic DNA, and the wavelength of individual experience, which is your consciousness fingerprints. We now insert the additional chorus track that allows consciousness to interact within the various galactics and the games they create. This new track relates to the analogy of the radio station band and tuning.

The additional track is the wavelength of the galactic consciousness to which the fragment is sent. This allows the fragment to exist within and observe the unique galactic bandwidth. Without this adjustment, it would be the same as the radio in your vehicle attempting to connect to the FM band while tuned to the AM frequency. It won't see the FM band and doesn't know how many channels exist there or the content of those channels unless it has been tuned to interact with it. Once the fragment's bandwidth is set, it can interact with the entire spectrum of stations that exist within the target galaxy. We must now fine tune the frequency so that it can interact with the specific station—Earth construct, era 2018, version 27. This brings us to a discussion of timelines and history.

CHAPTER EIGHT

THE RELATIONSHIP BETWEEN TIMELINES AND HISTORY

We hesitate to broach this subject because of the inordinate amount of focus placed upon this construct. We could start and finish this entire topic with a one-sentence definition:

"Time is the filing system that humans use to catalog their experiences."

From our perspective, this completely sums up the arbitrary concept that you consider as time. In the myriad connections established with human consciousness, one question always arises: When will |insert anticipated event| occur? From our perspective, we cannot make exact calculations of which events will transpire or the moment in your existence when they will occur. The construct you operate within is but one version in a multitude of constructs that consciousness is co-creating. To us, these versions appear as shimmering golden auras surrounding the planet, one within the other. Each aura is a version of the construct that exists apart from the others, and every one of them operates under the probabilities of decisions that will be made by the consciousnesses participating in them. Consider the number of people that exist upon your planet at this moment. Now consider that action and reaction between them are intertwined to form the next series of events that occur. From this, you may understand our reluctance to answer these questions because as a collective, you are literally creating your own future from one moment to the next.

We now will integrate your time and history concepts into the perspective we see from our vantage point. While there are many versions of games in play on Earth, we will only discuss their general interrelationships.

THE TIMELINE CONCEPT

You exist in a reality where recorded history leads you down a path that ends in your modern times. These catalogued events have happened a certain way and cannot be changed because they are in the past. This view backward that you see from your reality is the timeline in which you exist. Using the radio station analogy again, consider the timeline you are viewing as a distinct channel to which you have tuned your receiver so that you can interact with it.

The past you see behind you exists only on this station. Conversely, the future you all co-create also only exists on this station. You exist within a single, golden shimmering aura of frequency among the multitudes on Earth. To understand how consciousness interacts with these various timelines, we shall relate this to a similar concept you have created.

Many of you engage in virtual games and play through online connections. These games have waiting rooms where individuals collect until there are enough players to start a game. Consider that these players also can drop into a game already in progress anywhere they want. They cannot set the original parameters because the game already has begun, and they have no effect upon what already has occurred. This directly correlates to a consciousness wanting to experience a specific timeline. It incarnates into that timeline within the presented window of opportunity. A dizzying array of timelines now exist on Earth, but this was not always the case. Everything has an inception point, and timeline constructs are no exception.

THE FIRST TIMELINE DEFLECTION

We will begin our focus at a point where the Earth sphere has cultivated second-density consciousness and is ready for third-density consciousness to begin its incarnations. Recall that organic consciousness began as a single photon and now has ascended in density to the point where it is ready for its first incarnation in third density. First and second density still exist, but a new creation must commence to continue the expansion of consciousness. We now observe tribes of humanoids just beginning to understand the concepts of third-density embodiment. While difficult to comprehend, this timeline still exists, and if you are an organic planetary consciousness, you will have had at least one incarnation in this setting to lay the foundation of third density. This timeline of basic existence continues as the only third-density construct, until a portion of the organic third-density planetary consciousness has incorporated these lessons. With its consciousness sufficiently expanded by the construct, it now is ready for something more.

This is where an event or series of events occurs that causes a deflection, the timelines split, and then there are two versions of the construct. The originating timeline still exists and remains the basic-training section for the first-incarnation third-density consciousness. The new timeline contains additional experiences that will allow continued expansion for the budding consciousnesses. This new timeline will progress until the level of consciousness dictates another deflection, at which point three constructs will exist upon the material sphere of Earth. This is the formula of ascension. It is not a singular trajectory of a finite amount of consciousness but a continual process through which organic consciousness enters and ascends. This can be likened to your school systems on Earth, where an endless stream of children enters for their education and exit as functional participants in your creations.

We now will equate this to the radio frequency analogy. Remember that as you choose the games with which to interact, your frequency must be aligned to observe and interact with that specific construct, and each galactic consciousness wavelength is considered as the band of the radio (AM, FM, SW). The originating timeline would be considered the lowest station to which you could tune on that galactic bandwidth. When the first deflection point occurs, the frequency on your radio has left the original station and is now tuned to the next station that has just been created. There now exist two stations on the galactic Earth bandwidth. This process continues until the energy created by the collective begins to push back upon the galactic energy web.

Timeline "Eras"

Some misconceptions exist regarding timelines. As you can see from the above discussion, timelines diverge at **specific** points when conscious ascension dictates it. We add emphasis to the word specific intentionally. Each version of the Earth construct that is in existence contains a span of experience for consciousnesses to learn within. These span what you would consider an "era"; for example, the Roman era, the Medieval era, etc. These are large spans of experience that exist within your concept of time. They are fluid and ever changing, with scenarios dictated by the decisions made by the consciousnesses incarnated there. As different consciousnesses incarnate in the timelines, they gain the knowledge and once again reach the deflection point. It is here, as a collective, that they decide which path that deflection takes, and once again another unique channel has been created. As an individual consciousness, you can choose your experiences within the chosen timeline, but you do not singularly dictate the course of the collective consciousness. You may be a powerful force in your timeline and affect a large portion of the collective consciousness, but the collective ultimately decides.

Once the deflection occurs and the new timeline exists, the view backward into past events becomes solidified; the timelines have diverged. While the previous one still exists, the new timeline no longer observes it because it has moved into the new construct built upon the solid foundation of past events. You will not be able to travel into the past construct and change the foundation of this unique construct. You may possess the technology to shift between the timeline frequencies, but you will not be able to influence the events of the timeline in which you exist by traveling to a previous one.

With these concepts understood you can imagine that numerous timelines have now diverged from past timelines that still exist on Earth. Another concept related to the inclinations of individual consciousness is as follows: A consciousness that has had an impact on a specific timeline will want to incarnate into the future timeline that contains the history in which it participated. Assume that you were Augustus Caesar during the Roman era. Looking back from the timeline in which this book exists, you can see he had an impact on the course of that era. You can be assured that even though the consciousness that was Augustus may not remember his exploits in that lifetime, that consciousness will want to incarnate in this timeline because he helped create it.

THE APPROACHING DEFLECTION TO FOURTH DENSITY

We now arrive at a discussion of the current timeline and what we are observing. From our vantage point we can see that the timelines are once again about to diverge. In your New Age communities, there is much discussion surrounding the Earth-splitting concept. The definitions vary, depending upon the source, but as you assimilate the previous discussion on the operation of timelines, you may now understand what everyone is attempting to describe. The consciousnesses existing as a collective in this timeline are reaching the deflection point and are about to create a new timeline. When this happens, the consciousnesses that possess the density, experience, and desire will shift into this new timeline while the existing timeline remains. Consciousness that is not ready or is unwilling to shift will stay in the current timeline. This is the shift to fourth density, and it is long overdue for this collective. This timeline shift and ascension to fourth density is a separate event unrelated to the ending of the negative polarity experiment in this galaxy.

Let's overlay the topic of negative polarity onto the concept of timelines and history. Up to this point in the collective histories of Earth, negative polarity has existed, and its influence has created some interesting events. Your observed history is rife with brutal conflicts and, with few exceptions, conquest was the precursor to peace. This division from unity was the reason negative polarity was created, but it has outlived its usefulness and is being phased out. The question, then, is how will this affect all the timelines that exist upon Earth and throughout this galaxy?

The answer is easy: Negative polarity will no longer exist in any construct anywhere in this galaxy or any other.

As we stated, all timelines that exist have a history that was solidified when the deflection occurred. These histories can be likened to a photographic image that is forever locked upon the substrate at the moment of capture. Any timeline that was created from the carnage of negative polarity will contain the history of that carnage, but from that moment forward in the construct, division or hatred will no longer exist. It is easy to see the conflicts that negative polarity currently creates in your reality. Now imagine that all traces of negativity were removed from your timeline from one minute to the next. What would that look like? With no impulse or desire to inflict harm upon each other, what would you do? With the focus no longer on self-serving interests, how quickly will your reality change?

This will also happen in all the other timelines that currently experience negative polarity. The Viking and Roman eras will no longer be eras of conquest. Whatever they become without negativity will be decided by the collectives that exist there.

Time and Consciousness

We must clarify the observation and relationship of time to consciousness. Multiple timelines and eras exist upon Earth, and consciousnesses can choose where they would like to incarnate. In that regard, the singular linear progression of time, as experienced through history, is not absolute. The futures of each of these constructs are based upon the probability of actions undertaken by the collectives that exist there. Consciousness incarnated in these constructs exists within a space-in-time (space-time) as you are locked into the linear progression of events that occur there.

This does not infer that as a disembodied consciousness, you exist at all points simultaneously. By this we mean that you are not a single-photon, first-density microorganism **and** a completely ascended galactic consciousness. There is a linear progression to your ascension through the densities. If you began as a first-density consciousness, you will ascend through the densities in the manner previously described. When you ascend far enough that you contain a surplus of density, you may decide to fragment and reexperience a lower density, and your consciousness will then have concurrent experiences. During the concurrent experience of fragment and higher aspect, the original consciousness still observes a linear expanding density. This is the nature of the cosmos, and this linear progression of consciousness is known as "time-in-space" (time-space) because outside material embodiment, everything exists within an ever present **now**. Refer to Figure 12, which is discussed in detail in Chapter Ten.

To add perspective to the linear progression of consciousness, we will relate this to the observable cosmos. From your vantage point on Earth, you clearly observe the continuous expansion of galaxies and the universe. As previously stated, the observable galaxies and the universe exist as separate toroidal spheres of consciousness, whose increasing photonic densities create the observed expansion. This quantifiable effect occurs outside of your space-in-time relationship, yet there is an observable linear progression. In the ever present now of time-in-space, the expansion continues. The universe did not begin and end simultaneously because there is no observable time; the universe began as a void that continues to expand under increasing density… as are you.

CHAPTER NINE

UNDERSTANDING COLLECTIVE CONSCIOUSNESS

Up to this point, we have defined individual consciousness and alluded to the concept of collective consciousness. We have gradually helped you step into a greater understanding of the cosmos where you exist. As you engage with this book and assimilate the concepts, the information assists your expansion. The pyramids of Egypt have stood for centuries and still inspire awe, yet each began as a sturdy foundation upon which the blocks were laid. This book is that foundation in consciousness.

We have defined consciousness, the way it gains density through experience, and how that frequency of experience is unique to each consciousness. We also have shown the progression required for it to ascend through the games until it ultimately joins a collective consciousness. We must now discuss the construction and operation of the collective to which you aspire.

THE BEGINNING OF COLLECTIVE CONSCIOUSNESS

Look around your current construct. Do you see the beginnings of collective thought anywhere? Of course you do, because that is the natural tendency of positively aligned consciousness. Due to the influence of negative polarity, you also see attempts to create division and all its submanifestations. Negatively aligned consciousnesses do not pursue collectives, the very nature of this polarity is to divide and inhibit such actions. Instead, you will observe negative polarity creating hierarchal power and control structures that serve self-interests. During this discussion, we will ignore the negative structures and instead will focus on the positively aligned budding collectives.

These observable groups are forming because the consciousnesses have common goals and objectives. Regardless of the goals these groups pursue, they are the beginning lessons of collective intent. Expanding our view, we see that although the group is focused upon a singular objective, the individuals that comprise it have other interests separate from the group objective. This, in simple terms, is how an ascended planetary collective operates.

An individual consciousness that has ascended through fourth density into the fifth no longer has the need for physical embodiment. Simply stated, there is nothing left to learn from these experiences, and the next level of consciousness expansion involves lessons dealing with collective interactions. This does not mean that an ascended consciousness won't want to embody again at some point, but we already have described the fragmenting concept, and that is how that will occur. In fourth density, the lessons of collective intent are emphasized and expanded upon. While this begins in upper-third density, as seen from the above examples, the concepts expand exponentially. During early fourth-density embodiment, the individual consciousnesses continue to coalesce and globally align to common goals.

As the collective grows and consciousness begin to unify and focus on a common objective, the power of this collective is felt. The manifestations of their intentions occur with increasing speed, which then reinforces the desire to operate in unison. These goals tend to focus on the welfare and consideration of the species as the focus on the self falls away. We previously stated that the energy and nature of photons is such that there is a natural tendency to form adhesions. During embodiment, these adhesions manifest as a unified group. The power of this unified group continues to grow until a single planetary collective exists. The potential this unlocks within creation and the abilities that become accessible require extensive practice to use correctly. These are the lessons of fourth density. As consciousness graduates into fifth density, the lessons of the collective turn to sympathetic coresonance and harmonic waveform amplification as they become a true collective consciousness. With this overview of what occurs from an observational perspective, we will now discuss what occurs at the photonic level.

THE SCIENCE BEHIND COLLECTIVE CONSCIOUSNESS

The foundation of any collective is that they all contain the same photonic base wavelength. Recall that when organic first-density consciousness is created from a galactic consciousness it contains donated photons. Every photon of consciousness created within a galactic will contain the respective galactic base wavelength. As the created consciousness ascends in density the natural tendency to form adhesions exists because they are all aligned at the same base wavelength. The universe has a repeating nature, and we will describe this tendency using an analogy that exists within your sciences. We will incorporate several concepts into this discussion of individualized consciousness to bring an understanding of how an individual can become part of a larger collective, while maintaining autonomy.

It is well known that atomic structures contain energies both of attraction and of repulsion between the constituent components of the nucleus. The energies of attraction are called "binding energy," and when this energy exists in abundance, related to the repulsive forces of the protons and neutrons within the nucleus, the atom is considered stable. The photons of consciousness operate under similar principles, using a different energy structure.

The binding energy of photons is a constant, naturally occurring force. Within an individual consciousness, the binding force exists inside the barrier membrane of individuality. This holds the photons securely in a tightly packed array as the entity increases in density. As the consciousness continues to increase in energy and density, the repulsive forces associated with the energy contained in each photon, which we termed electromagnetic repulsion, attempt to push them apart (Figure 8). The binding forces are overwhelming, however, and this push-and-pull action, in concert with the spin of the individual photons, begins the toroidal rotation previously discussed. This pushing and pulling during rotation also creates energetic oscillations. The unique energy signature created by both the oscillations and the energy contained within the photons create a frequency unique to each consciousness. This oscillating frequency is their signature consciousness wavelength. We now see these forces operating together to create the energy of ascending consciousness.

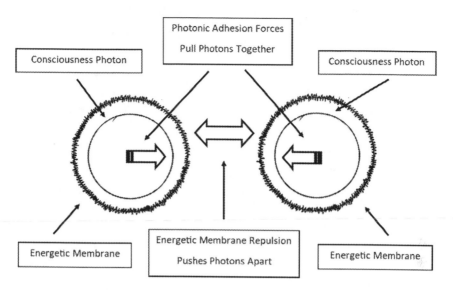

FIGURE 8
The Energies of Consciousness

    Two photons within a consciousness array are simultaneously pulled together by the photonic adhesion that naturally exists and pushed apart by the electromagnetic emissions created by the energy contained within the photons. This pulling and pushing creates oscillations within the rotating sphere of the consciousness. The energy signature created through the unique action of rotation and oscillation creates the frequencies of individualized consciousness. On a cosmic scale, the electromagnetic emissions created by individual consciousness photons is the source of creational energy throughout the cosmos. Everything exists within the God Source consciousness, and this unlimited energy permeates the universe. This is the source energy used within planetary collectives to create interactive *etheric* energy constructs.

In first- and second-density consciousness, the energetic membrane is weakly formed by the energy content of the photon. In third density and beyond, this unique oscillating frequency creates a strong energetic membrane that surrounds the entire structure and protects the information within it. This membrane and the photonic energy within it is what makes you a unique entity in the vastness of the cosmos. The membrane can be considered a shell that then protects the energy signature of the aggregate photons comprising the consciousness. As this consciousness ascends and joins the collective, the membrane continues to encapsulate the photons of the individual. It is now an individual consciousness within a larger toroidal sphere of collected consciousnesses. All the other individual consciousnesses that have organically ascended through the construct have the same perspective; they observe themselves as individual within a larger whole. This occurs through the sympathetic action of the base wavelength they were created with and the resonant action of collective intent.

In an individual third-density toroidal sphere of consciousness, we described each photon as rotating because of the interaction between the binding and repulsive forces. With this picture in your mind, expand the toroidal sphere, and instead of a single photon as the constituent particle, replace it with the toroidal sphere of a self-aware consciousness (refer to Figure 6 or 7). All the individual consciousnesses have now joined to form a massive toroidal planetary consciousness, termed a "collective consciousness" (Figure 9). With an understanding of what a collective is, we must discuss the interrelationship between it and other concepts.

Everything rotating within a galactic construct is balanced carefully within a consciousness energy web. This energy balance continually changes, based on the ascension of consciousness within the systems of matter. This requires continuous energy-balance calculations, as the energy created from the forming collectives increases. Upsetting that balance can cause distortions to the energy web and degraded planetary orbits and potentially can cause collisions of material creations.

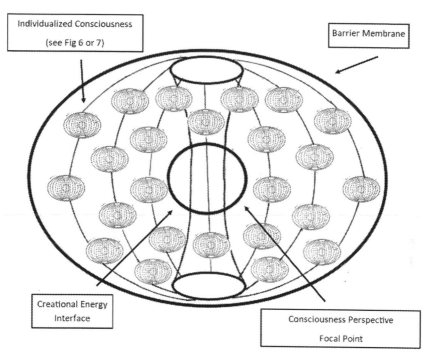

Individualized Consciousness
(see Fig 6 or 7)

Barrier Membrane

Creational Energy
Interface

Consciousness Perspective
Focal Point

FIGURE 9
Collective Consciousness Geometry

A collective consciousness maintains the same architecture as individual self-aware consciousness. The individual consciousness spheres assume the positions that photons occupy in a consciousness sphere and begin rotation. The collective has control over creational energy and creates the construct in which they will interact within the magnetic barrier of their collective. As individual consciousnesses ascend into the collective, the sphere increases in size and power. Each individual consciousness that joins the collective must contain a balanced energy and rotation, or it would induce a wobble within the collective architecture.

As previously discussed, one of the methods used to balance systems that produce large amounts of energy is to collapse the star and allow it to return this energy directly instead of transmitting it through the galactic energy web. When it becomes evident that collapsing the energy star of a system is required, ascension through the first and second density is halted. All the timelines that exist at third density and above are then allowed to ascend into the collective. Deflection points within the timelines begin to resolve themselves as the originating third density incarnations ascend through the timelines, and their respective eras end.

A planetary collective, then, is not just the consciousnesses with which you currently are embodied but every consciousness that has ascended through any of the timelines that ever have existed. Understand that collective consciousness requires collective intention and alignment. Negatively aligned consciousness ascending into disembodied existence cannot be assimilated by a positively aligned collective. We offer this statement only for clarification because negative-polarity consciousness is soon to be an obsolete construct that requires no discussion.

EXISTENCE WITHIN THE COLLECTIVE

Before we begin our discussion of collectives, we must define the term we will use to describe the energy that collective consciousness connects to and creates from. This energy exists between the photons of consciousness from which the collective was created, as represented in Figure 8. In the early days of scientific discovery on Earth, physicists observed the interactions of particles and attempted to mathematically quantify the results at which they arrived. As they did this, they noticed errors in the calculations and concluded that the particles were interacting with an unseen force that they could not measure. In these early experiments, they created a variable to balance their equations and termed it the *ether*, which was based upon the Greek word *Aithēr*. This ether was considered the base constituent of the universe and filled that which was presumed to be empty. As science progressed, the concept of ether was discarded, and the idea of something filling the voids would later become dark energy, dark matter, and other concepts that are used for advanced technology.[6,7] The term ether, however, stuck and is currently used in awakening publications to describe consciousness that works with energy existing in the "ether-ic." We will use this accepted term, but this is an energy that we previously defined and not a mystical force. Again, what you call a thing is of little consequence.

All consciousness—collective or otherwise—uses the energy of the consciousness within which they are immersed. For example, as you read this text, your consciousness exists within the planetary collective of Earth. When you meditate and focus upon drawing energy into your consciousness, you use the energy of the planetary consciousness you reside within. The planetary consciousness, in turn, uses the energy provided by the system consciousness, which uses the energy provided by the galactic consciousness. All galactic consciousnesses use the unlimited energy provided by the universal God Source. In all cases, they operate within the electromagnetic energy created through the interaction of the photons that comprise that consciousness. As they gain density and become collective (Figure 9), they can increasingly manipulate this energy and create their realities. For our purposes, we will identify this space of existence and the energy it contains as the *etheric*.

The first thoughts that an individual consciousness has when envisioning the collective consciousness is that it will be assimilated and lose its individuality. This same fear arises when some consider the ending of their current incarnations. You have a lifetime of experiences that make you who you are in the body you have now. What will happen to the individual that you have come to know as yourself when the body ceases to function? The simplest answer to that question is that you are still the same person you think you are now. The more encompassing answer would be this: Who you think you are now has a lot to do with who you have been before. Disregarding the ego programming required to operate in the chosen era, you will continue to have a conscious awareness, the same as you do reading this text. You also will remember reading it. To put existence within the collective into proper context, let's describe it using an event at the forefront of everyone's thoughts—the ending of this incarnation.

When your embodiment ceases, there is an initial disorientation as you find yourself conscious with senses you think are associated only with the body, except there is no body. During this time, an etheric construct will be created for you, and one or more entities will be there to help you reorient yourself. The transition is meant to be comforting, peaceful, and without fear. Therefore, what you see and who you meet there depends on what you expect. If you follow a religious doctrine, one of the entities will appear as the deity you expect and will help you understand the transition. If you were a Roman and expected to enter towering marble buildings in the afterlife, they would be there for you. Beyond the visuals observed is the reality—an energy construct created with conscious intent. The mechanics of what we just described are as follows for an organic third-density consciousness.

Your consciousness was untethered from the body when it ceased to function. With the anchor released, your consciousness is energetically attracted to the planetary collective consciousness. As the barrier membrane of your consciousness reconnects to the collective, one or more beings from the collective welcome you and create the etheric construct you expect. Etheric energy constructs are like what is created when you dream, except that a direct untethered connection allows a higher order of energy. With the assistance of the energy of collective intent, the construct you enter will seem as real as the one you exist in now.

Expected afterlife construct aside, this is the experience of existence within a collective consciousness. As an assembly of consciousnesses, you have the sympathetic resonant action of collective focused intent. This allows the collective to manipulate the creational energy web within the galactic consciousness. They then create a world within the etheric and an energy body that exists within it. From a galactic viewpoint, we see this collective as a rotating toroidal sphere comprised of individual consciousnesses, forming a single organism. Within the sphere, however, the individual consciousnesses still observe themselves as separate, operating within the agreed-upon construct and interacting with other individuals. Everyone reading this book has had at least one morning in which he or she woke up surprised to find that what felt so real was just a dream. This is the reality of the collective construct; the only difference is that you are in conscious control of it.

CHAPTER TEN

THE INTERRELATIONSHIP BETWEEN TIME, DENSITIES, AND DIMENSIONS

To show the relationship between the timelines, densities, and *dimensions*, we must show the interrelationship between variables. Again, the purpose of this book is to expand consciousness, not provide scientific theorems. We discuss these concepts in generalities, and as a collective you may explore and expand upon them.

We provided an overview of time and the fact that there are different interpretations of it. From an ascended perspective, there exists an ever-present now of time in space or *time-space*, in which consciousness undergoes continual expansion. During embodiment, however, your consciousness is locked into a specific space in time, or *space-time*, through which it will observe and learn. All space-time constructs that exist for embodiment are created using a unique vibrational frequency of matter within which the construct will solidify. We previously described these as stations on the band of a radio to which you tune your consciousness. The closest approximation to this concept in your accessible sciences would be the analysis of phonons[8] and harmonic lattice dynamics[9] found in quantum theory.

Within your current construct, you measure and calculate the movement of particles through the four dimensions that are quantifiable, three dimensional locations in space, and a time measurement. The arbitrary speed of a light photon is used in a two-dimensional scale of speed and time—but not mass—as the object moves and the coordinates are calculated. This is a direct representation of an object locked in space-time. This object moves within a discreet timeline, observable by embodied consciousness. Particles that cannot travel faster than the speed of light are contained within this space-time lock (Figure10).

Photonic consciousness operating in time-space can connect with another consciousness instantaneously and share information, regardless of distance, because it operates outside the confines of a space-time lock.[2] Consciousness is a rotating toroidal composite of photons, and the entire structure moves beyond the limitations of the gravitational constraints that occur in space-time. Since photonic consciousness operates outside of space-time and within the creational energy web, it can be inferred that quantifiable light photons also can move beyond the dimensional space-time lock, once you understand the mechanics involved.

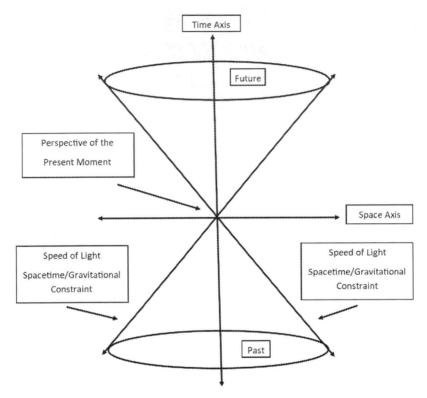

FIGURE 10
Boundaries of a Space-Time Construct

The illustration above represents the accepted four-dimensional model of space-time presented by Hermann Minkowski.[14] The two cones representing past and future intersect at the current space and time axis. Consciousness locked in this space-time construct travels along the intersection of the time and space axes and can observe events within the cones, giving the linear perspective of past and future. Photons of light are observed as constrained by the speed of light, and this is represented by the outer edges of the space-time cones. This graph represents a single space-time construct that is solidified within a specific frequency and wavelength and held in place through a gravitational lock that occurs as solidified matter moves within the galactic consciousness.

TIMELINES

Multiple timelines exist on the planet; they are separated by the frequency and wavelength in which the structures of matter are solidified. The frequency and wavelength of the construct is a function of the energy contained within the solidified matter. These three-dimensional space-in-time lattices are held in place through the employment of the gravitational waves (resistance to motion) that occur as the solidified matter interacts with the constituent photons of the system consciousness, which is within the galactic consciousness; ultimately, everything is within the God Source consciousness. Without falling into the well of endless quantum theory equations, consider the timelines as separate three-dimensional boxes. Viewing these individual timeline boxes (Figure 10) as slivers on a space-time graph, we arrange them within the coordinates of increasing frequency and wavelength. As the frequency of the construct increases, there also will be a resulting increase in vibrational wavelength. As this occurs, you are then able to stack one four-dimensional reality on top of the other. Each four-dimensional space-time is a complete construct unto itself and does not bleed over at the edges (Figure 11).

To define this concept of boundaries, consider the smallest currently observable particles that have been identified through your destructive collider events at CERN (European Organization for Nuclear Research).[10] These collider events are currently observing the creation and decay of fragmented particles.[11, 12] If energy (not beam acceleration) was added to these particles, rather than watching them shed energy as they seek stability after impact, you instead would see them increasingly vibrate and spin until they disappeared. The answer to the question that should then be sought is, "Where did they go?"

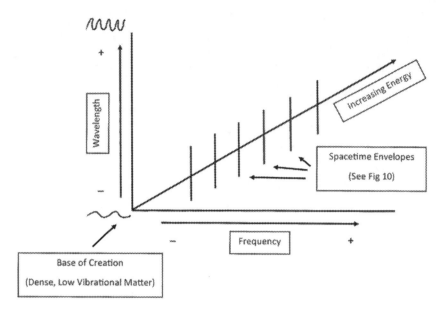

FIGURE 11
Stacking Space-Time Constructs to Create Timelines

The above graph shows the direct relationship between increasing energy and the increasing frequency and wavelength of separate space-time envelopes. As the creational energy is increased within the constituents of matter, they will vibrate at a higher frequency, which in turn increases the oscillating wavelength of observable matter. Turning the space-time envelope shown in Figure 10 sideways, individual space-time envelopes are stacked one over the other as the energy within them increases. As the energy solidifying the matter in each space-time increases, the density of the matter decreases.

Conscious Density vs. Space-Time Density

The discreet ascending space-time constructs we have just described have been numbered and labeled in various communities as dimensions or densities. Calling these constructs *dimensions* can lead to confusion when you consider that multiple constructs exist for each density of self-aware consciousness. Similarly, calling the constructs densities confuses them with the definition of the density of consciousness, which is required for ascension. They are more appropriately termed "timelines within a density of consciousness."

As previously mentioned, all planetary spheres exist within a fixed-base wavelength. This is the baseline frequency/wavelength and is observable throughout all the constructs. This is also the densest construct, due to the length of the waveform and the low frequency. As the timelines diverge and continue up the scale of wavelength/frequency, they become less dense because of the increasing frequency of the creations. This is where the term density became related to diverging timelines. It is correct in its literal interpretation of what occurs, but diverging timelines are created by the increasing density of the consciousnesses in that timeline. We can visualize this by creating a graph of density vs. time-space and trending the density of consciousness and the density of the timelines simultaneously. This is the same as the discussion of evolving organisms; consciousness evolves and therefore drives the change. The increasing density of consciousness and the associated decreasing space-time density of material creation is the correlation that allows an expanding control over the constructs (Figure 12).

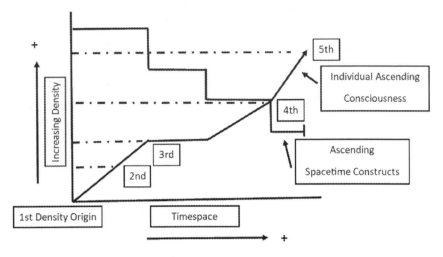

FIGURE 12
Consciousness Density vs. Space-Time Density

The graph above shows the relationship between the ascending photonic density of consciousness and the decreasing density of matter, within the space-time envelopes within which they experience embodiment. As consciousness ascends, the collectives of an existing era create a new timeline that diverges to begin a new era of embodiment. The new timeline creates a new space-time construct (Figure 10) that is solidified using a higher energy. The more energy contained within the solidified matter, the lower the density of the space-time construct. First- and second-density consciousnesses are placed where they are needed within the various constructs, and the linear progression shown is for ease of understanding.

Conscious Density vs. Time-Space

We have discussed the densities of consciousness and how they determine the architecture of the toroidal sphere of consciousness. As the sphere progresses in density and complexity, increasing abilities are activated that allow control and manipulation of creation. As you increase in density, you embody in timelines that provide higher lessons of responsibility and service to the collective until embodiment is no longer required. The lessons then continue as disembodied consciousness within the planetary collective in time-space. If we place this concept on a graph of density vs. time-space, we see that consciousness originates in first density at the axis and begins its progression in increasing density. When the consciousness arrives at third density, it requires several incarnations before it learns its lessons and increases to the fourth density. While this occurs, there is a passing of time-space. This is the representation of ascending consciousness from a single photon (Figure 13).

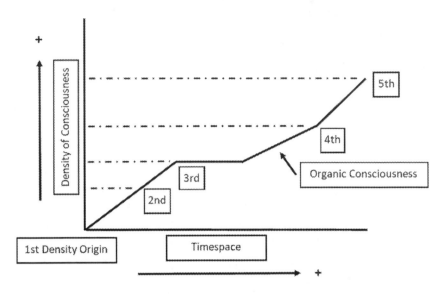

FIGURE 13

The Linear Expansion of Consciousness

This graph is the relationship between the increasing density of consciousness and the perceived existence of that consciousness in the now of time-space. The consciousness originates as a single photon in first density and begins the process of acquiring the experience needed for ascension. As it moves through the densities, a distinct measure of time-space has elapsed. As the consciousness moves from the need to embody in space-time, it then will exist solely in time-space, and the measure of time-space continues to accrue.

This does not infer "time," as it is recorded on Earth. It is meant to illuminate the fact that consciousness does not exist at its origin *and* at its completely ascended component simultaneously. To emphasize this point, consider that scientists are observing the Universal Consciousness undergoing continual expansion; this is occurring in time-space.

Putting all this together in one graph, we see that an organic consciousness originates at first density and ascends through a single space-time density until it reaches self-aware third-density consciousness. As the lessons become more involved, it takes three incarnations in a single space-time density and one in an ascending space-time density before it is ready to ascend into fourth-density consciousness. Two incarnations in separate ascending space-time densities are required for the entity to reach fifth-density consciousness, where incarnations in space-time are no longer required. During the experiences of embodiment in space-time, time-space continues to be calculated and is linear (Figure14). This represents a highly condensed view of ascending consciousness for illustration purposes only.

This is the nature of consciousness. It begins at first density and ascends through incarnations as it learns lessons through experience. There will be as many incarnations as required to learn the needed lessons in a specific density. There is no time limit, and outside of your incarnations, there is no perceived time. As the graphs imply, however, a linear progression of increasing density is occurring in time-space.

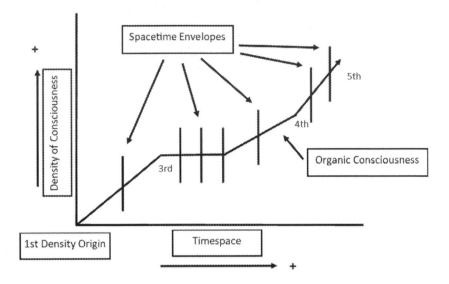

FIGURE 14

The Ascension of Consciousness through Embodiment

This graph represents the ascension of organic consciousness through the space-time constructs. In a highly condensed example, we see that the consciousness ascends through one space-time envelope to reach third density. It then requires three successive incarnations in a single space-time envelope and one in an ascending envelope to reach fourth density. It then requires two incarnations in ascending space-time envelopes to reach fifth density.

THE MECHANICS OF SPLITTING A TIMELINE

As we have stated, consciousness can see from its density back downward, therefore the planetary spheres and first and second density are observable from your current perspective. What happens to these lower-density creations is a function of what you, as a collective, are co-creating. As timelines shift, the lower densities shift with you because they are part of the construct and are manifested by your needs within the timeline. This is a confusing concept but one that needs to be explained to remove any paradox concerns.

First- and second-density consciousness are placed within a timeline where they are needed. Their toroidal sphere has not yet attained the architecture of a self-aware entity. Therefore, it does not matter which timeline they are in because the experiences are generic in nature. As timeline shifts occur, the lower density consciousnesses are reshuffled, and this can occur through various mechanisms. First density consciousness is a basic creation, and whatever structures exist in the new timeline are repopulated with new consciousness. Because second-density consciousness is at a higher level of development and has undergone duality pairing, it requires more consideration. The creation of a diverging timeline is not an unexpected occurrence and is therefore carefully planned. Leading up to the shift, second-density consciousness whose incarnations end will be held back from another incarnation until after the shift. This does not mean that second-density incarnations end; they are, however, scaled back, and this manifests as species extinctions and lower birth rates. The other method employed is a die-off that occurs within one or both timelines as they diverge. When the shift occurs, second-density consciousness is then shuffled between the timelines as required.

The other question that requires an answer is how planetary spheres exist throughout the densities without showing signs of overlapping timelines. Digging a gold mine in one timeline does not create a hole where the gold has been extracted in another timeline. The planetary spheres have been created and placed within the energy web of the galactic consciousness. Their core frequency must exist at the base wavelength to be locked within the web to create the rotational resistance that produces the gravity constants of space-time. From there, we must again consider the repeating nature of the universe and look to our prior discussion of photonic consciousness. Planetary spheres contain more than one track of frequency in the same manner that photonic consciousness contains the recording tracks that compose the symphony of individuality. As the timelines shift, so too does the planetary construct with which you interact. As stated previously, whatever planetary changes have occurred up to the moment of the shift will be maintained. Whatever happens to the planetary surface after the shift in the two diverging timelines will be observed only by the respective timelines because the planetary frequencies that solidify the matter have changed with the timelines.

To visualize this, imagine the molten core of your planet as the base wavelength emitter. This spinning mass of electromagnetic slush is what locks the planet into the spatial energy web of the galaxy. The physical layers of the planet that exist beyond this base wavelength can then be considered another track on the recording. These tracks are unique to each timeline that exists upon the planet and have been created by the decisions of collective consciousness that are manifesting that timeline. The discussion of energy grids and vortex points that exist upon the planet relate directly to the timeline frequency track. This grid and vortex point system allow for a seamless overlay of the shifting timelines and provide the energy nodes to shift the construct. The only limit to the number of timelines that can exist on a planet is the energy of collective consciousness that increases to the point of upsetting the energy balance within the galaxy. A planetary collective can be held back from ascending if it ascended quicker than expected or if a planet in the offsetting quadrant underperforms.

Chapter Eleven

SHARING GALACTIC CONTENT AND GALACTIC AGREEMENTS

The observable galaxies operate within the unique wavelength of each galactic consciousness. Individual consciousness must be realigned to match the various galactic wavelengths if they desire to experience the unique creations found in them. We will use generic terms to describe the complex interactions of electromagnetic frequencies and wavelengths and their impact upon self-aware consciousness.

Realigning Individual Consciousness

We have previously described the various frequencies that a consciousness contains—the base wavelength, the experience wavelength, and the gaming wavelength. The base wavelength is a function of the originating source photons that was termed "photonic DNA." This track is unchangeable and allows reintegration with the donor source of the originating photons. The experience track is what was previously termed "consciousness fingerprints" and is what makes you unique. The gaming wavelength is what an individual consciousness who wants to play in the games of another galaxy must have realigned to experience the other constructs.

When traveler realignment has been agreed upon, both galactic consciousnesses begin the process of realigning the wavelength of the consciousness. This is accomplished through a frequency tunnel that slowly realigns the consciousness involved. The mechanics discussed may seem impossible with the current technology available on Earth and the inferred distances observed, but from our perspective, it is like reaching out and holding hands. Remember that the cosmos exists within the toroidal sphere of God Source. With this understanding and the repeating nature of the cosmos, we state that the galaxies are held within the conscious energy web in the same manner as systems are held within the galaxies and that the space between galaxies is far from empty.

The frequency tunnel is created within the energy web of God Source and can be described as a swirling whirlpool of photons that forms from each of the respective galaxies. The whirlpools are large vortex points that originate at the top of the toroidal galactic spheres. As they reach out to each other, the swirling tunnel narrows continuously until a small pathway connects the two. As the transported consciousness moves through the narrowing conduit, its gaming frequency is slowly neutralized. By the time it reaches the narrow connecting portion, it has been zeroed out. As it travels through the expanding portion of the other side of the conduit, it is slowly realigned to experience within the receiving galaxy. Additional fine-tuning will be required inside the new galaxy before it can observe and experience the various games offered there.

To visualize this realignment concept, imagine an elongated hourglass with the narrow center connecting the two glass globes. The consciousness traveling through the hourglass tunnel is the sand. As the sand travels down one globe toward the center, it begins spinning faster and faster as the dimension decreases. When it reaches the center, it spins so fast that there is no observable motion. This relates directly to the frequency and wavelength of the traveling consciousness. As the sand exits the narrow center, it again begins an observable spinning motion, but now the spin is compatible with the spin of the other side of the globe. As the sand exits the hourglass, it now spins in harmony with the spin of the receiving galactic consciousness. The consciousness then is ready to be fine-tuned to play in the desired constructs within this galaxy.

Sharing Galactic Content

The cosmos is not a haphazard jumble of wandering matter created from a singular big bang. The cosmos was created and is managed under intelligent design; the intricacies of movement and order should illuminate this fact. Within the ever-increasing energies of the cosmos, merging is becoming more prevalent between large galaxies. During the early stages of creation, the galaxies easily operated and existed within the fabric of the God Source energy web. As the galaxies grew in size and power, the energy balance became more complex. Additional corrections became necessary to preserve the positioning and rotational dynamics of the universe. One of these balancing actions is to merge galaxies that then become an energy anchor. Other methods are employed to correct small imbalances, but the cosmos has reached a stage of expansion where larger corrections are needed.

The merging of galaxies is observed from your density, and you calculate the outcome of the combined components, based on the constituent elements. Is there enough matter to form stars? How will the rotations of dissimilar galactic orbits be impacted? The answer is that it depends on the composite upon which the two galactic consciousnesses agree and the energy-positioning requirements to maintain integrity. The merging of these observable galaxies is not a haphazard occurrence but a carefully orchestrated event to preserve the integrity of the physical creations. To facilitate a smooth transition, a sharing of content is established prior to merging that allows the ascended collectives the ability to meet and communicate. The sharing between galactic consciousnesses occurs through the employment of the hourglass tunnel previously described for sharing individual consciousness. The difference in this case is that the creation of the tunnel is permanent and is the precursor to a complete frequency change of both galaxies as they become a unified consciousness. As the galaxies move closer to each other, the tunnel between them becomes shorter and larger in diameter. If you were able to observe this, it would appear as single-cell organism division in reverse.

The passing of existence for a galactic consciousness is not measured in the same manner as an embodied consciousness locked in space-time. From this perspective a merging observed from Earth that appears to take millions of years is experienced by a galactic as a continuous process of weaving planetary rotations and gravitational effects. Merging is a complex and highly coordinated endeavor and is an experience sought by mature galactics.

When a merging is planned, the first consideration is for the systems that contain embodied consciousness. These must be preserved, with any effects from the merging eliminated or reduced to minor inconveniences. The creation of constructs through which consciousness can ascend is a lengthy process, and every attempt is made to preserve them. There is also an investment of love and nurturing given to each creation, the same as raising a child on Earth. If there are any rotational degradations, planetary impacts, or ejections of matter from the respective galaxies, they are required to maintain the overall balance and preserve inhabited systems.

The galaxy in which Earth resides is in the early stages of merging with a neighboring galaxy. The tunnel that allows sharing has been established, and ascended consciousness has been traveling between the two galaxies. We state this to illuminate the control each galaxy has on the sharing of content. The realignment that occurs as consciousness or matter moves through the tunnel from one galaxy to the other is not automatic, and an unauthorized consciousness that attempts to transit faces the loss of identity.

Unauthorized Transit between Galaxies

As stated, the galactic consciousness in which Earth resides created negative polarity to force positively aligned consciousness to strive to overcome the separation that negativity creates. After careful observation, negative polarity was considered a poor experiment, and it is being eradicated from this galaxy. Opening the tunnel between the Earth galaxy and its neighbor has allowed ascended consciousness from your neighbor to be brought to bear against the negative infection. This does not mean that negatively oriented consciousness also can use this tunnel to escape into the other galaxy. The connection is closely monitored, and negative polarity is easily identified.

Assume that you have dug a tunnel beneath the frequency fence that divides you from your neighbor on Earth. You have done this so that your family can easily move between the two properties without having to climb the fence. This also allows your family to bring with them the tools that might be needed, instead of leaving them behind as they scale the fence. The tunnel is convenient, but it also could allow a thief to enter your property just as easily. Because of this, you agree to stand guard at the entrance to the tunnel so that only your family enters the tunnel. Conversely, on the other side, your neighbor also agrees to stand guard to ensure unauthorized personnel do not exit. Now assume that each family wears an easily identifiable but unique perfume. This perfume is strong, and you can smell it long before anyone enters the tunnel. Regardless of outward attempts to obfuscate appearance, the perfume is unmistakable, and anyone who smells different is not part of the two families.

The above is a simple analogy of what is currently occurring at the connection between the two galactic consciousnesses. If a negatively aligned consciousness attempts to transit, it will be immediately identified and neutralized. Since photonic consciousness cannot be destroyed, we use the term neutralized in its purest sense. A negatively aligned consciousness carries the construct of negative polarity within itself. This is the reverse rotational photonic spin previously described, and it manifests itself as intentions that oppose God Source unity. Let us assume that a fully aligned negative consciousness attempted to transit the connection between galaxies. This is an unwise decision and would not be attempted, but we will use it as a thought experiment.

Traveling toward the narrow portion at the center, a negatively aligned consciousness will feel uncomfortable as its frequency and vibration are accelerated. As it reaches the center of the narrows, one or both galactics will transmit an overpowering pulse of positive energy into the consciousness. This would remove all traces of negativity from the consciousness as it realigns the photonic energy and completely erases the accumulated experiences. The decision would then be made into which galaxy the consciousness would exit. Since this consciousness no longer has any memories or experience, guides will meet it that will assist it. Any photonic density beyond third that this entity carries will be shed as it is reintegrated into the beginning of third-density embodiment to reacquire lessons and experience.

CHAPTER TWELVE

ASCENDING COLLECTIVES ATTAINING GALACTIC ABILITIES

Now that we have sufficiently assured everyone that they will retain their unique barrier membranes of experiential identity, it is time to describe the singular instance where this is voluntarily surrendered.

During the early existence of this universe, galactic consciousnesses were directly created from God Source. There initially were twelve, until these became fruitful and began returning the energy donated for their creation. When sufficiently recharged, God Source created another twenty-four galactic consciousnesses. The cycle continued, and another forty-eight were created. The exponential building of conscious energy in the cosmos continued unabated in this manner. During this expansion, the organically ascending collectives within the first twelve galactics successfully acquired the energy and balance to become the initial galactic graduates. The universe within which we exist is currently at an energy level where direct galactic ejections from God Source have ended. New galactic consciousnesses are being created through the graduation of collectives, which we now will describe.

Thus far, we have described the electromagnetic barrier membrane that protects the unique identity of individualized consciousness. This barrier remains intact as the individual ascends beyond the need for embodiment into the planetary collective. As ascension continues within the collective, the energies of consciousness and collectivity increase until a threshold is reached. At this level of collective energy, the lines of individuality begin to blur and the need to create etheric constructs to interact within falls away. This is a clear sign that the energies of the collective are approaching unity with the creational energy web of God Source. As previously stated, unfiltered, prolonged exposure to the power of creational energy will realign the energy signatures of individual consciousnesses as they are overpowered. This is what occurs within the collective as they voluntarily ascend in energy toward graduation. When graduation occurs, the entire composite is realigned to a unique base wavelength that now becomes their galactic signature. They are then positioned within the unfiltered energy web of God Source consciousness and are free to begin creation within themselves in any manner they desire.

This is the concept eluded to in the various discussions related to returning to Source. The reality is not the stated objective of being reabsorbed and reunited with God Source. This concept, literally interpreted, would mean the dissolution and loss of all acquired energy and experience. This is in direct contravention to the purpose of ascension. The reason for existence and experience is to ascend and become a contributing member within the energy symbiosis of the cosmos. Graduation to a galactic consciousness achieves this stated goal and immerses the graduating collective directly within the energy web of God Source consciousness. In that regard, you have become one with Source because you now are fully ascended and have direct access to the power of God Source. The most wonderful part of this journey is that none of the individual experiences of the collective has been lost. The perspective after merging is of a single consciousness that has the experiences of the entire collective. This is the same concept as an ascended consciousness creating a fragment of itself and then merging once again to become a single consciousness.

To understand what occurs, consider the oscilloscopes that exist to measure voltage waveforms. This device creates a visual representation of multiple oscillating waves generated by A/C voltages on a display. Separate voltages are shown on this display in relationship to each other and the waveforms they are creating. Assume the oscilloscope instead monitors the waveforms of three individual consciousnesses within the ascending collective. Three unique energetic waveforms appear on the screen. Each consciousness contains the energy of experiences that brought them to their current ascension level. The displayed waveforms represent this uniqueness by appearing as waves of differing heights and duration. As the energies of the collective continue to increase, the three waveforms slowly align in both height and duration until they match each other and resonate in unison.

Now extend this example to include every consciousness that exists within the entire system of consciousness. This is a similar principle to individual consciousnesses needing the lessons of experience to achieve a balanced toroidal rotation before they can join the collective. With balanced rotations firmly established, the last requirement is that the collective must resonate at the same harmonic energy signature to graduate. From your current perspective, this discussion appears to infer the loss of identity and may seem undesirable. At this level of consciousness, however, the loss of individuality is no longer a concern, and graduation to a galactic consciousness is a highly sought experience.

Graduation to a galactic consciousness involves the entirety of consciousness that has been created within a system consciousness, including the system consciousness itself. Consider a solar system that contains four planets, where consciousness will ascend through the densities. Before the first photon of life is set upon the planets, there already exists a system consciousness and four planetary consciousnesses that oversee the subsequent creations. As life ascends through the densities of embodiment on the four planets, they join their respective planetary consciousnesses. When the power of the collectives reaches the required threshold, new creations on the planets are halted, and the remaining consciousness within the densities ascend until all reach their collectives. With no embodied life left within the system, the collectives continue their respective ascensions in energy and density until they have attained the same threshold level of energy and resonance between each other and the system consciousness. The four collectives are then drawn into the system consciousness. A unified collective consciousness now exists where previously there were five— four planetary and one system consciousness. It is here where the final stages of alignment occur before being ejected from the galactic consciousness into the energy web of God Source. This is an incredible achievement and a wonder for all galactics to behold.

DISSOLUTION OF UNNEEDED MATERIAL CONSTRUCTS

After the amalgamation of the collectives with the system consciousness, the planetary spheres of matter and the compressed energy star still exist but are no longer useful. The planets may be reabsorbed through the center of the system consciousness, if there is a need to do so. This is a simple process effected by increasing the spin rate of the compressed (black hole) material, which in turn increases its gravitational effects and pulls in the nearby planetary constructs. This increases the mass of the compressed (black hole) material, and the process continues until all the unneeded material has been reabsorbed. Alternately, the planets may remain in an orbital rotation, if needed for balance, within the originating galactic consciousness. They also may be set upon their own trajectories, scheduled for destructive impacts, or ejected from the galaxy and left to wander the cosmos until they dissolve.

PART 2

OPERATING IN CONSCIOUSNESS

CHAPTER THIRTEEN

We thus far have provided a foundational understanding of the operation of the cosmos within which consciousness operates. It is important to understand the basic architecture, so the concepts of consciousness can be viewed with the proper perspective.

THIRD-DENSITY INCARNATIONS

The toroidal sphere of self-aware consciousness is established at the entry into third density. The definition of self-aware is that the individual begins to operate beyond the instinctual programming of second density and questions his or her existence and ultimate death. The first incarnation in third density is in one of the earlier organic timelines, where the basic behaviors of human existence are presented. These first lessons come in the form of a primitive tribe, where the requirement of cooperating to survive is reinforced. This also allows the consciousness to become acclimated with the capabilities and limitations of the human vehicle.

Regardless of whether you are a graduating second-density consciousness or a fragment from an ascended consciousness, if you have never been in a human vehicle, you must experience at least one of these basic lifetimes. When this first incarnation ends, your consciousness will be met in an etheric construct of your choosing. If you do not have an expectation of the afterlife, a peaceful setting will be created for you. This is where one or more fourth-density consciousnesses will assist you in understanding what you are, and the lessons you require to become a responsible and capable consciousness. You can choose to experience these basic constructs as many times as you deem necessary, but most individuals are eager to move on to more challenging experiences as soon as they are able.

The timelines and the lessons they contain become increasingly detailed as you ascend in conscious capacity. Look at the world you inhabit; complex interactions occur between consciousnesses that bring intricate lessons to each of you. It is easy to look back through recorded history and observe that the farther back you go, the simpler the interactions were. This is a direct correlation to the increasing complexity of the lessons of consciousness. From a reactionary viewpoint, you may dismiss the increasing complexity as a by-product of scientific exploration and discovery that has built upon itself over the generations. This again ignores the fact that the manifestation of increasing consciousness pushes this visible result. Consider that the ability of telepathic communication is commonplace in fourth density. Does it then make sense that you are preparing for this development by walking around with electronic devices that mimic this ability?

Levels of Consciousness and Perspectives

Eras of time contain ascending levels of experience; so too do levels of consciousness exist within those timeline eras. Again, observe the world you inhabit. A separation of awareness and abilities becomes clear if you know what to look for and understand what is driving it. Consider a consciousness incarnated here who has just graduated from a simpler timeline. The complexity of this timeline can easily become overwhelming as it attempts to learn and adjust to the new conditions. Myriad distractions exist, and it requires some discipline and experience to navigate along the chosen course. Several forms of assistance are offered, one of which is to be born into a religious family, where the doctrines provide a rope with which to pull oneself around the distractions that exist. With every opportunity to help a consciousness find its way, free will ultimately allows consciousness to make its own decisions while incarnated. Even bad decisions offer a lesson, and they impart a deep energy signature upon the consciousness.

While incarnated, you have a clear idea of what you want your life path to be, based upon the influences that shaped your operative ego thought process. As consciousness before incarnation, however, you may have had a completely different perspective. While you have no memory of it in this lifetime, assume that the two prior incarnations contained lavish experiences of wealth and privilege. You have never experienced a lifetime of struggle, and this is an experience you need for a complete perspective. Embodied in the lifetime of struggle, you now observe, through this experience, the disparity of wealth from the opposing viewpoint and understand the inequality and hardship it creates. While you live this lifetime, it seems unfair that you would have such a difficult life; no one should have to experience this. When the life ends, you find yourself in the etheric with your guides, and you will understand why you chose this for yourself—it was required to provide energetic balance. Since everyone currently observes incarnating entities as born with a blank slate that is then drawn upon, there is a misconception that all consciousness starts at the same level of experience. This brings us to a discussion of the veil of forgetfulness, why it exists, and how it can be thinned.

THE VEIL OF FORGETFULNESS

This is a misunderstood concept that has been associated with any number of negative scenarios, none of which is true. The truth of this construct is much simpler in design and reasoning; it was created to allow ascending consciousnesses the ability to repeatedly experience lower densities and less-evolved timelines. The formulation of a well-rounded consciousness that contains the proper lessons of experience requires repeated incarnations. The veil allows you to "pretend" while you are incarnated that you do not consciously remember prior lifetimes and the experience they provided. Assume you were born into this incarnation with thousands of years of experience gained through your lifetimes. What would be the point of the lifetime if you already knew what you were here to learn?

To reinforce this concept, consider that you are walking down a wooded trail on a bright sunny day. You can clearly see all the trees, avoid any obstacles in your way, and know where the trail turns and forks. Now assume that you are on the same trail on a moonless night with a small candle. Navigating the trail has become considerably more difficult and, by the same measure, that much more rewarding when you successfully navigate it. From this perspective, you begin to understand that the veil of forgetfulness is a construct that was created to help and assist you.

Assume that a third-density consciousness has completed an incarnation and has passed through the healing and remembering process. It now plans the next lifetime with its fourth-density guides. This consciousness is close to ascending into fourth density but missed a few lessons it had scheduled in the previous lifetime. With the next lifetime planned and the embodied insertion point defined, the next step is to erect the veil of forgetfulness.

Third-density consciousness exists as a rotating toroidal sphere that stores the energy of experience within the matrix of its constituent photons. As previously described, a swirling whirlpool connects to the top and bottom of this sphere. At the center of this column is a bulge that represents the seat of consciousness. As you read this book, you perceive your awareness as located just behind your eyes and associate this with your brain. When your incarnation ends, this perception of awareness will exist at the bulging center of your toroidal sphere. Variations to observed perspective can occur as consciousness, but for this discussion, assume the center.

The veil of forgetfulness is more appropriately described as a frequency partition that has been erected within each individual toroidal consciousness sphere. With your seat of consciousness at the center of your sphere, imagine that a spherical barrier has been placed between it and the remainder of your toroidal sphere. The outside of the sphere continues its rotation, and a separate rotation commences inside the partition. You now are effectively a fragment inside your consciousness. This fragment will acquire the construct programming known as ego.

When you are born into a body on Earth, it is within this partition that you begin to learn and grow under the illusion of amnesia. As your life progresses and you mature, the veil expands as you increase your photon count and energy within it through experiencing life. As this occurs, knowledge from previous incarnations can sometimes bleed through. What you can access depends on the energy signature of your prior knowledge and how focused you have been on expanding your understanding of consciousness. This is defined as "thinning the veil."

Erecting the veil of forgetfulness is accomplished in the etheric of the collective using frequency generators that create a photonic barrier within your consciousness. These appear as four small golden balls of energy that encircle the periphery of your toroidal consciousness. They rotate 180 degrees apart, forming an X, and begin to spin. As the spin increases, it realigns a portion of your photonic array into an energetic partition. At the point where this partition is solidified within your consciousness, the spinning orbs are moving so fast that they appear as a golden bubble encapsulating your consciousness. The partition starts at the center of your consciousness and is expanded to just beyond your seat of consciousness (Figure 6). As this occurs, the energy of prior experience is pushed outward, and the consciousness now observes itself as a clean slate that is waiting to be written upon. You are now a fragment within your larger self. This process may appear undesirable and cruel from your current vantage point, but as soon as your incarnation ends, you will want to do it again. For when the veil is removed, you will have all your experiences back, and you will remember how much fun it is to pretend to forget.

To understand the concept of the veil, consider that you have just purchased a new computer to replace an outdated one. Its hard drive has the capacity to store more information than is needed at the time of purchase. This is a learning computer, and as you begin to use the programs that operate it, they write themselves upon the hard drive. You also have data on the old computer that you want to keep separated from the new information. Since you have more than enough memory on your new computer, the best way to maintain separation is to partition the hard drive so that one set of information will remain separate from the other. This is the veil of forgetfulness, and it has been erected within every third-density consciousness that exists on Earth. In addition to the veil, there also is the concept of shedding density, which was outlined in a previous section. These two concepts, when used in conjunction, allow the density of consciousness to be realigned to learn lessons in any construct.

KNOWLEDGE BLEEDING THROUGH THE VEIL

For various reasons—some planned, some through the desire of the consciousness—abilities can be brought forward into successive lifetimes. For example, consider the lifetime of the composer Wolfgang Amadeus Mozart. At the age of five, he was playing piano and composing music, and he spent the rest of his life becoming one of the most revered composers of his time. Now assume you are the consciousness of Mozart and are planning your next lifetime. Unless these abilities are shed through a density reduction, it is almost certain that in the subsequent incarnation, this consciousness again will embrace these musical talents as its energy bleeds through the veil. The talents may not manifest in the same manner, but the ability to play and compose music will come easily to the new incarnation. Intense experiences from previous incarnations often bleed through the veil due to the energy they contain and the desire of the consciousness to reacquire them. This phenomenon is observed as children who exhibit unusual abilities in art, music, or sciences at an early age. Again, some of this is planned, and some is through sheer force of will. Free will is respected, and there is no judgment if you access prior experiences through determined effort and no judgment on how you utilize them. If accessing certain talents, however, has the potential to impede your lessons in this lifetime, they will remain inaccessible.

DEATH OF THE BODY; ENDING OF AN INCARNATION

Did you just pick this book off the shelf at the bookstore and flip to this page? There are many who will, and that is understandable. The ending of an incarnation in third density is the transition through a doorway into a new existence, of which little is known.

Since the second trimester of pregnancy, your consciousness has been tethered to the body with which you currently identify. This was not a random act; you chose this body and the family you are a part of. When the body functions cease, the tether releases, and your consciousness is pulled toward the planetary collective. It is here that you will be met by one or more guides, who will help you with your transition. If you follow religious doctrines and expect one of your deities to meet you, this will be provided within the etheric reception area construct. There is a period of disorientation as you begin to understand that the senses you previously associated with the body—sight, sound, sensation—still exist but are no longer corporeal or limited in perception. As you enter the reception construct, you are assessed and, if necessary, prescribed whatever healing you require.

If your death was abrupt or against your will, either by accident or through the actions of another consciousness imposing its will upon you, a period of understanding and healing will be required. If you were closely following the planned life path or were firmly entrenched in living a powerful life when it was cut short you may need to continue along that path in an etheric construct. This allows the perception that you are still incarnated in that lifetime until you accept that it has ended and are ready to move on.

Creating a realistic environment in the energy web of the etheric plane is accomplished through the power of collective consciousness. Many millions of consciousnesses currently exist within the planetary collective of Earth. This collective consciousness surrounds the planet and can be envisioned as a golden shimmering aura just beyond the limits of the gaseous atmosphere. When a consciousness ends an incarnation, it connects to this collective, which previously was defined as a swirling toroidal sphere, composed of individual consciousness spheres of the same architecture (Figure 9). The energy this collective wields through unified sympathetic resonant intention far exceeds anything that can be manifested during embodiment. Creating a realistic construct within the collective for a disembodied consciousness is an easy task that is performed repeatedly as incarnations end upon the planet. These etheric constructs created for healing and transition can be likened to a dream that is more real than any dream experienced during incarnation. Dreamscapes during incarnation are created at a lower energy level accessed by the subconscious, and as real as they may seem at times, they do not compare to these etheric constructs.

Having completed an incarnation on Earth and successfully reorienting your consciousness to disembodied existence through the reception construct, your veil of forgetfulness must be removed so that you have access to your complete experiences and can make decisions related to your future path.

The veil of forgetfulness is a frequency partition that has been erected within your toroidal sphere. Removing this partition is accomplished in the reverse order previously described for its creation. As the partition dissolves, it will feel as if your consciousness is expanding to meet the spinning orbs you can observe outside of you. Your consciousness will feel electrified as the fog lifts and the true extent of your experiences returns to you. What happens after this depends upon where you are from and what you will do next.

THE EGO CONSTRUCT

The misunderstood idea of a separate ego construct and what happens to it when an incarnation ends causes undue anxiety because of the varying interpretations that are available. Because of this, an inordinate amount of attention has been given to this relatively simple creation of consciousness. To put this into perspective, let's observe three stages of growth: infant, adult, and geriatric.

INFANT

Look into the eyes of a baby, and you can see the awareness of consciousness that exists within him or her. The baby may not be able to talk, but there are times when you can almost hear what he or she is thinking. This is the underlying consciousness that exists before the programming of the lifetime has commenced. Consciousness can experience any number of timelines—on Earth, within this galaxy, and anywhere else within the cosmos. Incarnating into the myriad unique constructs requires operating protocols specific to them. The operating protocols that are acquired are worn over the underlying consciousness and can be likened to clothing. This clothing that allows you to interact and seamlessly mesh with your chosen construct is what has been termed ego on Earth, but it is more appropriately termed *operative consciousness.* The power of the underlying consciousness to direct the course of the life once this programming has been established is a function of how balanced the toroidal sphere of consciousness has become from previous incarnations.

ADULT

Moving forward in a lifetime, we find consciousness has become an adult, with all the required programming complete and in effect. Whether the ego programming is all-encompassing and provides the singular focus of life is again a factor of how developed the underlying consciousness was prior to this incarnation. It is during adulthood that the clash between the acquired programming and the underlying conscious intention will be felt—if it is felt at all. Third-density consciousness that have few prior incarnations will grasp firmly upon the ego construct as they attempt to use it for guidance, as they can feel no other steering force. Ascending consciousness, however, will identify the ego programming for what it is and step away from what is no longer useful, as it feels the internal current of higher consciousness. It then will weigh the programmed desires against higher-order goals, and the upward trajectory becomes clear. Ascending consciousness can feel a higher order of balanced, conscious energy behind the veil of forgetfulness earlier in life. At what age it begins to steer is a function of magnitude and lessons chosen for that incarnation. A discussion of shedding the ego will be provided later in the book.

GERIATRIC

Moving forward once more, we now find this entity nearing the end of the incarnation. Having lived most of the lifetime, this is the period of reflection and review. Where the entity finds itself will depend largely upon whether the ego survived the battle of higher consciousness intact during adulthood.

If the ego has been the driving force of the lifetime, it will consider itself the only aspect of consciousness. The course of the lifetime will reflect the programming acquired and the surrounding environment experienced. The lessons scheduled to be learned by an inexperienced consciousness will be few and will revolve around one or two major events in the lifetime. The ego will be fixated upon the ending of the lifetime and what portion of itself, if any, will survive the transition. Fearing the loss of identity, many ego-bound consciousnesses embrace religions with a single-life narrative, where the ego construct is assumed to continue forever in the described afterlife.

If the higher aspect of consciousness was felt during the lifetime, the amount of ego dissolution will depend upon the magnitude of balanced consciousness available and the willingness to embrace it. Assuming the higher aspect asserted a moderate influence, the perspective from this position in life will be one of acceptance. This consciousness understands itself to be the active portion of a larger whole involved in acquiring experiences through life. From this vantage point, it will begin to seek additional lessons that might fill any perceived gaps in experience. If meditation has been practiced with any consistency, it is well acquainted with its underlying consciousness and can clearly see the division between ego programming and its true identity. Any fear associated with death that remains will be a result of the veil of forgetfulness obscuring the previous transitions. Several methods can be used to further thin the veil during an incarnation; they will be discussed later in the book.

THIRD-DENSITY ORGANIC CONSCIOUSNESS

The term organic is used to differentiate between consciousness that originated as first density and ascended into third density and ascended consciousness that has fragmented and is playing in the games of Earth. There is no hierarchy in this terminology. It is used as contrast between the two, and nothing more should be inferred.

When a third-density consciousness is in between lives, it interfaces with an upper fourth-density consciousness that appears as it expects. If you have no expectation, you may observe one or more glowing orbs that communicate with you. Again, your comfort and acceptance are critical, and if you resist or disbelieve, you will find yourself in a healing construct until you understand and accept what has occurred and where you are before the next steps are taken. Assuming you accept what is happening, your guides will help you with a review of your previous life, once the veil of forgetfulness has been removed. Whatever lessons you had scheduled in that lifetime will be observed and the results assessed. We must stop for a moment and define the term "lessons," which is another idea that conjures a host of negative connotations within a consciousness immersed in the polarities of Earth.

The required lessons are not punitive in nature but are for your benefit and assist to make your consciousness a balanced component of the larger collective. We previously spoke of the contrasting lessons of wealth and poverty and how both perspectives are required to provide balance. From this example, it is easy to see that without the contrasting experience, you would not understand the action and reaction caused by this inequality. This would create an energetic imbalance within your toroidal energy sphere, and you would polarize toward the singular experience and resulting emotional charge your consciousness experienced. These balancing experiences, or lessons, are required to give you the proper perspective and energy so that when you are ready, you can seamlessly join the collective.

Assume that lessons were no longer required and that energy balances and perspectives within a consciousness were disregarded. From this point forward, if you had attained the density of consciousness to ascend into fourth density, it was automatic. With all the discussion in this book related to energy balances throughout the cosmos being of paramount importance, what do you think would happen?

Assuming unbalanced collectives could form, they would be composed of consciousnesses with singular experiences on myriad subjects. It would be difficult to arrive at unified thought and direction, considering the varying levels of experience contained within individuals who comprise this collective.

When viewed from an ascended perspective, the toroidal sphere of this unbalanced collective would appear to be undulating, with large peaks and valleys as the sphere rotated. This would be an ineffective collective, since unified sympathetic resonant intention is critical to the ability to manipulate the energy web of creation. Increasing the energy of this collective would result in ever larger oscillations until the energy either would have to be reduced, or the collective would have to be disbanded and remediated. Conversely, a well-organized and aligned collective toroidal sphere would be observed as a perfectly round sphere whose rotation is precise. As the energy of this cohesive collective increases, the rotation gains speed, and the sphere increases in diameter. The addition of balanced individual consciousnesses ascending through the densities would continue unabated until this collective attained galactic abilities.

From this discussion, we hope that you begin to understand the purpose behind the lessons of experience and that they exist to help consciousness grow into responsible, well-balanced creators. The deeper question is, "What is the purpose of stumbling around in the dark on Earth and being allowed to choose incorrect experiences?"

THE REASON BEHIND LESSONS IN THE DARK

We previously spoke of the satisfaction of finding your destination in the dark, but that is only a portion of the purpose. The concept of ego is well established and relates to the programming acquired during a lifetime. There also are discussions related to the dissolution of the ego and some mention of the higher consciousness that exists beyond the ego construct. This points to the fact that layers of consciousness are understood to exist. The concept of layers is what we would like you to focus upon as we discuss the reasoning behind lessons in the darkness. The essence of your existence is the photonic consciousness that is attached to your body. The experiences you have gained through your successive incarnations are stored as energy that causes the photons to vibrate, spin, and form a toroidal sphere. As you begin your journey in third density, you live under the veil, incarnating through successive lifetimes with no knowledge of your actual composition. As the lessons and lifetimes accumulate, you slowly become aware that there is an additional component internally guiding you.

Assume you had a previous lifetime where a drug or alcohol dependency led you away from your intended lessons and down a dark road. Although you may not consciously know why, in subsequent incarnations you will have an internal compass that steers you away from these distractions. The cause of this observed effect is the balanced energy of your photonic consciousness providing the inertia that precludes the pull of this distraction. If this is a lesson that required several incarnations to learn, when you do begin to feel it, the aversion will be overwhelming. This occurs beyond your operating consciousness, but the effects are still felt. This simple example exposes the purpose and result of learning lessons under amnesia. As the energy of these experiences begins to balance the toroidal rotation of your consciousness, the effects impact your perceptions and thinking. When this balancing occurs, you are then set upon the path to your next experience, where your rotational geometry is fine-tuned to the next level.

To visualize this, imagine that a wheel on your vehicle has lost its balancing weights during a long trip. As you travel down the road, your vehicle shimmies and shakes from the vibrations caused as the unbalanced wheel rotates. Slowing down and reducing the rotation of the assembly alleviates some of the vibration and discomfort, but the wheel is out of balance and requires repair. At the tire shop, the technician puts the wheel on a machine that will balance it. If you watch closely, you will observe the technician spin the wheel, stop it, place a weight at the required location, and once again spin the wheel until another weight is placed. This process is repeated several times until at last the wheel spins true and does not cause unwanted vibrations. The wheel is then removed from the machine, and you once again proceed along your journey.

As you incarnate upon Earth and live your lives under the veil of forgetfulness, you have been placed upon the balancing machine of consciousness. When you have sufficiently learned a lesson, that experience becomes a balancing weight within your rotation. You then travel along with less wobble to the next balancing lesson. The true test of balance is your ability to navigate around the distractions toward experiences that uplift and enrich you, all the while oblivious that any of this is occurring. As you reach your destination in perfect balance and alignment, you are removed from the machine and allowed to proceed along your journey into fourth density.

BETWEEN LIFE REVIEW

Returning to our observation of a third-density consciousness that reviews its most recent incarnation, we find that it had hoped to attain several lessons that were needed for balance. These were the last lessons required before ascending into fourth density, but it appears that it missed the proper path on an important lesson in worth. The opportunity to choose the correct experience for this lesson presented itself on three separate occasions during the lifetime, but each time the incorrect path was chosen. This final lesson will have to be learned within the subsequent incarnation, which then presents the opportunity to fine-tune additional experiences that the consciousness feels would be beneficial.

To put this in perspective, consider the concept of divorce that some individuals experience repeatedly during a lifetime. Assume that this experience was chosen **by you** before incarnating to bring the lesson of humility and worth to you. This occurs through the capitulation of material possessions as you instead focus upon the value of the growing consciousness under your care. You have experienced two such divorces, and each time you relinquish custody of your children as you focus on the fight to retain your possessions. As your life continues, this lesson is brought before you for a third time. How do you respond as you once again find yourself at the crossroads of this experience? Do you level your shoulders at the obstacle and again retrace the steps previously taken? Or do you understand that the cosmos—which means you, outside of incarnation—is putting the same experience in front of you in the hope that you finally will see the path that leads upward and away from the cycle into the next experience?

In this discussion of lessons—and their repetition to provide opportunities to learn them—lies the trendy concept that all you must do is decide you want to walk a different path in life, and it will manifest in front of you. To a large degree, this is true, as you are the creator of your reality, and you have the authority to do whatever you wish with this lifetime. However, you must also understand that you came here to acquire experiences that you needed or to fulfill a specific role. If you allow the ego programming acquired in this lifetime to direct your course, you may miss the reason you incarnated in the first place. Joy and happiness are signposts along the journey to the next scheduled experience, and the truth of them can be felt in your heart. Even the divorce scenarios began with these markers. Therefore, follow those signs as you create your reality, and the correct path is assured.

PLANNING THE NEXT INCARNATION

Because a lesson was missed, there is still an energetic imbalance within the toroidal sphere of this consciousness that must be corrected. As the next lifetime is planned, ample opportunity will be provided to acquire the needed experience. Although the divorce scenario would have provided this experience and the resultant energy, any number of experiences can impart the same energy required. While the consciousness can repeat the same experience if it desires, a new interaction is usually chosen, rather than repeating something already experienced.

Each person reading this book has met others who, for one reason or another, stick with you and become lifelong friends. Perhaps you share a common interest, think alike, or have both experienced a common trauma. Whatever it is that brought you together has created a bond in consciousness and a shared energetic signature. These experiences can be considered energetic handshakes between consciousnesses that are easily recognized and create comfortable interactions when disembodied. This occurs through the resonant energetic wavelengths that exist in both consciousnesses and are easily transmitted through the collective. With this understanding, consider a third-density consciousness that has lived numerous lifetimes within this density. It has had intimate interactions with hundreds of other consciousnesses as it works through the balancing lessons of embodiment. As this entity ends an incarnation and once again finds itself on the other side of the veil, it will identify other consciousnesses in the collective with whom it shares the energy of experience.

As you understand the entirety of your experiences, you will plan the course of your next incarnation. A multitude of entities are doing the same thing, but those with shared energy signatures will easily find each other. Assume you recognize several entities as you prepare to chart your course. You have played together before, and the friendship exists, so bringing lessons to each other in the next incarnation is an easy decision. Due to the timing of incarnations, some or all of your previous friends may be involved in a current incarnation, while you are not, and for that reason, they will not be available to participate. The consciousnesses that you know in the waiting area, however, will be the ones who agree to bring you the deepest lessons of your next incarnation.

You have recognized four associates from prior incarnations, and all have agreed to participate in your upcoming life. For ease of understanding, imagine that the four of you now stand in front of the screens that will chart your respective paths during the next incarnation. You will select where you incarnate and what family you incarnate into, based upon the needs of the lifetime and how your interactions are planned. If one of your reunited friends was a younger sibling in a prior lifetime, and you protected him or her, that friend may agree to incarnate as your older sibling and return the favor.

The energetic bonds of love and intimacy are the strongest, and if one of your associates was a husband or wife in a prior incarnation, you can be sure that he or she will once again bring you a deep lesson. This could be in the form of a parent/child relationship, husband/wife relationship, or anything in between. These lessons may not always be viewed as positive during the incarnation, but they are necessary, and you both agreed to bring them to each other. With this perspective, all experiences should be reflected upon objectively and without the emotional involvement of ego. From that vantage point, you may then see the lesson the experience was meant to bring you, irrespective of whether you personally considered it good or bad when it occurred.

ACTIONS AGAINST YOUR WILL AND ACCIDENTS

This discussion of the perspective of lessons does not include actions that occur because of the influence and imposition of negative polarity against the will of consciousness. Imagine you are a balanced consciousness who has carefully charted its course through a lifetime of experience. This is your last incarnation in third density, and you methodically reach each of the prescribed lesson objectives. As you proceed along, your path randomly intersects with a consciousness deeply infected with negative polarity. For whatever reason, the polarity has manifested as a desire to kill, and it imposes its will upon your life path. There is no perspective to this lesson from the vantage point of the consciousness that has been killed, other than to accept it as unavoidable and finish the lessons in the next incarnation. There is, however, a very deep lesson that will ultimately need to be learned by the negatively aligned entity. From this perspective, we again state that negative polarity has been a poor experiment and has impeded the growth of an entire galaxy of consciousness.

While we are on the topic of external events that impact a chosen life path, it is prudent to address accidents. The definition of an accident is an unfortunate event that occurs unexpectedly and without deliberate cause. The systems of matter that exist and rotate within the galactic consciousnesses have been carefully balanced to provide optimum stability for the ascension of incarnated consciousness. Once set in motion, they are generally left alone, if the energy balance is maintained and unplanned extinctions do not occur. Orbital degradations occur for various reasons, and impacts set debris upon random trajectories. This is the normal order of the cosmos and is allowed to continue, unless the trajectories affect a planetary consciousness. In this case, a slight correction will be affected, and the object will continue along an altered path as the planet remains unaffected. Along with the complexity of rotational matter, billions of consciousnesses are incarnated upon Earth. Multiply that number by the habitable planets within a galaxy, and you will see the impossible task of attempting to prevent accidents from happening.

To put this in perspective, consider the galaxy and all consciousness within it as an elaborate game of marbles. The systems of planets are massive marbles, rotating and held within the fabric of the galactic energy web. The energy of this web is monitored, but minor fluctuations disrupt some of the smaller marbles, and as they collide, they shoot off in random vectors. If these random marbles do not threaten the marbles with ascending consciousness, they are left alone. Now consider the marble that is Earth. Upon Earth, you release marbles of embodied consciousness. As they set out along their respective paths, more and more marbles are released and the paths begin to intersect each other. As the marbles of individualized consciousness continue to increase in number, some of them randomly impact each other, based solely upon the volume of marbles in play. While most of marbles will travel unaffected to their destinations, some of them do not arrive. These are the marbles affected by accidents; some percentage of this is unavoidable and is accepted as a by-product of embodiment.

During an incarnation, the loss of a loved one to an accident can be devastating to the family involved, as they try to understand and move forward. This conversation is not meant to make light of the emotional burden that is carried by the remaining family members but to shed light upon the beauty of inextinguishable consciousness. While the incarnation may have ended abruptly, the consciousness has an eternity to acquire the needed lessons in subsequent lifetimes. Beyond the incarnation, the consciousness involved in the accident will view the event as unfortunate but not much more than a minor inconvenience. Because of the interruption, it may choose to wait for the remaining family members to finish their incarnations before it plans the next lifetime. This will allow it to plan the subsequent incarnation with the same consciousnesses that comprise the mourning family. During this time of waiting, it may also assist in guiding the remaining family members through their incarnations until they are reunited.

Returning to the area where you stand with four of your associates, consider that your life ended abruptly due to an unplanned accident. The four with whom you now stand were family members in the last lifetime. You decided to wait for them so that you could plan the next incarnation together and resolve the feelings of loss. While you waited for their incarnations to end, you helped guide them to the required lessons. This could have been in the form of dreamscape interactions, an angelic presence, or whatever interaction would have been best received by the still embodied consciousnesses.

With the incarnations ended and the reunion complete, each of you now stands before a screen upon which you will chart the course of the upcoming lifetime. Imagine that it appears as a map, with an originating point and a destination that equates to the birth and death of that embodiment. In between these two points, you will insert markers where important lessons are scheduled to occur. When these lessons are shared between you and one of your associates, your paths upon the screen intersect at that location. How long your paths coincide depends upon the lessons you have agreed to bring to each other. Arriving at this intersection to share the experience is entirely up to you and depends upon the balance you have achieved within your toroidal sphere of consciousness and your ability to avoid being sidetracked. Being able to correctly navigate to all the markers within an incarnation is the trait of a well-balanced ascending consciousness.

Your entrance into the chosen timeline has been selected and, along with it, the family you will become a part of. None of this is by chance; you selected your family based upon the emotional dynamics you will encounter, the genetic predispositions, and many other factors. There are concessions that must be made, and if there are aspects of embodiment you must have, you may have to accept a limitation in another area. For example, requiring a perfect body may mean that you accept a dysfunctional childhood, if you also need to be born within a specific location. All of this is accounted for, and you weigh the assets and liabilities of each perspective opportunity. You select one based upon your perceived ability to navigate the course, considering all the attributes of that incarnation. With the choice made, the veil of forgetfulness is erected, and you begin the wonderful journey toward your lessons with a perceived blank slate.

To understand the benefits of a blank slate, imagine that you are looking through a window at Earth. This window is covered with the grime of a hundred lifetimes of exposure to the elements. Your view of Earth through that window will be distorted by the accumulation and that view will skew your perceptions of Earth. Now imagine that the window has been cleaned to crystal clarity. With your view of Earth once again unobstructed, you are free to perceive the world with a fresh new perspective. This is what the veil of forgetfulness allows you, and it is for your benefit. It is a well-established learning tool that has been employed in thousands of constructs.

CHAPTER FOURTEEN

ASCENDING CONSCIOUSNESS, HIGHER CONSCIOUSNESS, AND THE CONCEPT OF FRAGMENTATION

We previously spoke of the concerted effort to overcome the negative polarity imbalance within this galactic consciousness. As a result, many ascended consciousness fragments currently are embodied on Earth. As the polarities continue to shift toward the positive, these fragments have enough photonic density and toroidal balance within them to almost guarantee they awaken from the ego programming. As this happens, they seek higher knowledge and purpose. The same is true of ascending third-density consciousness that has attained the density and balance to ascend within this incarnation. If you have been drawn to this book and have been engaged with the material thus far, there should be an intangible feeling that it is unlocking something within you. If that has been your experience, you fall within one of the following categories:

INDIVIDUAL FRAGMENTING WITHIN A COLLECTIVE

As you ascend beyond the need for fourth-density embodiment, individualized consciousness joins the planetary collective, where it exists as a part of the larger whole. The collective consciousness was described as a rotating toroidal sphere composed of individual toroidal spheres (Figure 9). It still observes itself as individual creating its own perspective, but it operates with collective intent for the good of the whole. The individual increases density through experience within the collective, and as it ascends in density, the lessons increasingly benefit all equally. As this occurs, the density within the individual grows to the extent that an excess of photonic density exists. At this juncture—a graduation point, if you will—the ability to fragment and create another portion of itself becomes a new experience it may pursue. The number of fragments that a consciousness can create is limited only by the density of the donor available for fragmentation, and the desire to do so.

The fragmenting of an ascended consciousness within the collective employs the same dynamic of compartmentalization as previously discussed. Since both the originator and the new fragment contain the same unique energy signatures within their toroidal spheres, the perspective will be one of duality. Both consciousnesses are now free to experience separately but are still a single consciousness. When the fragment completes its journey, the photonic density that comprises it will return and be reabsorbed by the donor. Since the base energy signatures are identical, the magnetic membrane of the fragment will dissolve as the photons are reabsorbed by the donor.

To better understand what is occurring, consider the mechanics of human hearing. You have two ears that are separate but work together to produce the binaural ability to detect the origin of sounds. Both operate independently, but their separate experiences are interpreted by your brain as a single event. Cover one ear, and it will have an experience unique to itself, while the other ear does not share that experience. The brain has recorded the experience regardless of which ear interpreted the sound. Now assume that each ear can be separated from your body and embark upon individual paths. They are still connected to your brain and transmitting data, but they encounter separate events. Since they operate in separate environments apart from the brain and each other, they are provided with the operating program (ego) appropriate to their respective paths. This allows them to independently maneuver through the terrain they wander. The separate paths ultimately end with the reunification of the ears with the head that contains the brain.

When reunification occurs, the ears do not tremble in fear at the loss of their operating programs, as you might expect. As the path to unification grows closer, they become increasingly aware that they are the brain and not the programming. The programming then falls away as thoughtlessly as a winter jacket during a journey from a mountaintop to a desert. As you drop the jacket because it is no longer required, you look back upon it from your new vantage point. With your perception of awareness still intact without it, you understand the consciousness that you identified as the jacket was underneath it. The jacket was nothing more than protection from the elements during that stage of your journey.

This is a fragment's creation and journey upon Earth in its present incarnation. The descent from the mountaintop is the awakening and realization of who and what you are. As you become aware of the jacket you are wearing, you also feel the constriction it creates on your larger awareness. This creates the drive to shed the restriction. Your search for deeper understanding and truth then commences in earnest. As previously stated, the awakening is a gradual journey of climbing the steps to an expanded view of the self and your relationship with creation. These determined actions thin the veil, and the continued work toward expansion will ultimately reveal your purpose for coming here.

Ascending Consciousness Perspective

At the current juncture in this timeline there are many consciousnesses undergoing the transition into fourth density during their incarnations. Many of these now-ascending entities were caught in the manifestations of negative polarity during repeated incarnations. This statement does not infer evil or nefarious intent by anyone or anything to purposely hinder the ascension of the collective. It merely means that the polarities have been skewed toward the negative on Earth during a large portion of recorded history. The polarities then made it difficult for consciousnesses incarnating here to avoid the distractions of self-serving interests. From an ascended perspective, these redundant cycles of incarnation on Earth look like a merry-go-round. Consider the following analogy:

Everyone picks their positions as the wheel of third-density life begins to turn. As the music plays and the carousel gains speed, the scenery begins to blur, and everyone forgets about everything except which horses they have chosen and whether they perceive themselves to be gaining on the horse and rider in front of them. The fallacy of this perspective is that everyone is riding on the same carousel, where there is no first and no last because you are traveling in a circle. The horses are, in fact, fixed upon the carousel, and the perception of movement is an illusion. Your turn upon the carousel of incarnation ends, and when the wheel comes to a stop, everyone changes position, based on which horse they perceived to be beating them during the last turn. The wheel of life then begins to turn again, and the cycle repeats. This has been the experience for a large portion of third-density consciousness as they repeatedly incarnated on Earth.

Ascending consciousness on Earth is now at a point where it has ridden the carousel of life so many times that it has begun to see the construct for what it is—an illusion. No longer dizzy from the polarities, it now looks beyond the rules of the merry-go-round as it searches for the path that leads it away from it. As it finds the path that leads it off the mountain and away from the merry-go-round, it too sheds its winter jacket of ego programming and encounters its larger consciousness that exists beyond the veil. The search for deeper understanding and truth is a universal ascending path that all follow toward enlightenment, once the awakening commences.

CHAPTER FIFTEEN

HYPNOTHERAPY AND REGRESSION; PERSPECTIVE ATTRIBUTED TO DENSITY OF HIGHER ASPECT

The silencing of the ego construct to contact the higher awareness of a consciousness is a practice that has existed on Earth for centuries. The methods and names have changed over time, but the underlying principle has not. This technique, when practiced as intended, allows the complete consciousness of the individual an unobstructed pathway to communicate. The term "complete consciousness" has more than one meaning when the context of higher self and totality of consciousness are compared. This context must be considered, as the information is provided. If you compare existing literature that describes the experiences of hypnotherapy clients, you will observe discrepancies in the perspective and content of the information. Some clients intricately describe the construction of a galaxy, while others can only vaguely describe their own experiences. In between these two extremes are an infinite array of alien life-forms—angels, dragons, star families, and planetary consciousness. As a result, the view described from the perspective of one client may seem to contradict the perspective observed by another. This does not point to a flaw in the concept of hypnotherapy but instead illuminates the validity of the practice as a consciousness-expanding modality. You need only to refocus your attention from the minutiae of the provided details to the overall cosmic perspective. To add clarity to this concept, consider the perspective a client would have under three separate circumstances.

THIRD-DENSITY ORGANIC CONSCIOUSNESS

We previously defined this as a first-density consciousness that has ascended through the densities and is now at some level of third density. It is working through incarnations, learning lessons until it acquires the density and rotational balance required to ascend. Since it has not yet mastered third density, it is not a fragment and does not have a higher component of itself to interface with. In this instance, when a session commences, one of two things will occur:

- If the client does not have extensive third-density experience, a connection to the complete consciousness will result in information useful to the expansion of the client. This would be along the lines of past-life traumas that affect the current incarnation or advice related to path correction toward lessons that have yet to be learned. It would not include information related to ascended consciousness or lifetimes alien to the Earth experience because it has neither.
- If the client has extensive third-density experience and has the photonic density to ascend but not the rotational balance, a connection to the complete consciousness will also include the assistance of a guide. The form this guide takes depends on what the client expects to see. Through the guide, additional details will be provided related to fourth density and the correct path needed to get there. While there may be some material related to fourth-density experience, it will be tailored to fit the knowledge level and understanding of the client.

ASCENDED COLLECTIVE CONSCIOUSNESS FRAGMENT

A client in this category can provide information that spans the spectrum. Earth is currently assisted by fragments from across the universe, so the perspectives and information provided will be as diverse as the cosmos itself.

Imagine that a powerful planetary collective exists in a system contained within a Galaxy on the other side of the universe. The call has gone out for assistance in correcting a failed experiment in another galaxy. Billions of individual consciousnesses exist within this collective and have long since ascended beyond the need for embodied experience, but during their embodiment, they were a race of what Earth would interpret as sentient blue elephants. As a collective operating outside of polarity, they are completely oriented toward love and assistance for all. They create their reality using the energy web and form etheric structures and energy bodies. Recall that a collective is a massive toroidal sphere composed of the individual toroidal spheres of the same architecture. The constructs they create for themselves to interact within in the etheric may not be recognizable to a consciousness immersed in the Earth experience. For this example, imagine an etheric construct has been created in the form of an auditorium, where a million individuals from this collective will gather. Since they remember their embodiment as blue elephants, that is the energy body they create for themselves in the etheric.

The steering committee of this collective stands before the crowd and tells the story of a galaxy struggling with an experiment called polarity. They look for volunteers willing to fragment and help this galaxy. It will not be easy, and you will not remember why you are there once you incarnate. You will have to work hard to awaken to your purpose, but it will be exciting and unlike anything you have experienced before. Moved by the speech, you raise your hand.

The hypnotherapist has just recorded a client telling this story during a regression session. He then asks the client what everyone looks like in this auditorium, and the client describes their appearance as shimmering blue elephants. She might relate her experience of coming to Earth through the perspective of a single consciousness. She might alternatively discuss the fragmentation process that created her, depending on what the client can understand. Now multiply this by the infinite number of collectives that exist and the diversity of life from which they ascended. The client, having connected to the larger portion of her ascended consciousness, now has access to information and technology relative to the ascension level of that collective. The information and the level of technical detail provided will depend upon the client's ability to interpret what she encounters and what is in her best interest.

These fragments have come here to assist in raising the consciousness of Earth and the ending of polarity. Considering the manifestations of destructive intention that still exist on Earth; capabilities that could be used in this manner will be withheld when connected to positively aligned collectives. For that reason, technical details and equations related to advanced theories will not be provided. Discussions of technology will be in generalities, but these descriptions will far exceed anything publicly known to exist on Earth.

PLANETARY, SYSTEM, OR GALACTIC-CONSCIOUSNESS FRAGMENT

With the understanding that the list above are all toroidal spheres of consciousness that have the capacity and desire to fragment, it is no surprise that some clients provide details related to being these objects. Rather than an exhaustive explanation, we will discuss what may occur when a consciousness embodied on Earth attempts to relate what it is viewing as the fragment connects to its source consciousness. The first consideration is that consciousness embodied on Earth has a lifetime of experiences that are limited to the creations and assumptions encountered during its incarnation. While it may be exposed to a larger view of creation as it is connected to the totality of its consciousness, the interpretations and perspective may be limited by its ability to comprehend what it experiences.

System Consciousness

Remember that consciousness perceives its awareness as originating at the center of the toroidal sphere, where the bulge exists between the two swirling pillars. A client who is a fragment of a system consciousness may connect to the totality of his or her consciousness and state,

"I am a star, and I am shining brightly."

The client has connected to the completeness of his or her consciousness and observes the perspective of that consciousness from its center. The star is only the focal point of that consciousness, and the grander view would be that the consciousness contains an entire system of planets within itself. The discussion that then follows will be directly attributed to the client's ability to interpret and accept what he or she observes. Alternately, a system consciousness that contains fully ascended operational collectives within it will not observe itself as an energy star because it collapsed as the energy of consciousness reversed through it. Without the glowing distraction at its center, the perspective of consciousness may then include a complete view of everything operating within it.

Planetary Consciousness

A client who is a fragment of a planetary consciousness will observe the world under its care because that is its primary focus. There is a distinct difference in the perspective of a planetary consciousness that must be addressed. A planetary consciousness is the initial consciousness imbued upon a newly formed construct that will be used for the ascension through embodiment. It is the photonic donor for the seeds of first-density consciousness that will begin to grow within that material sphere. As the seeds grow and ascend beyond embodiment, they join the planetary consciousness; this is the beginning of the collective. The planetary collective may consist of billions of other consciousnesses when the client connects to it, but the perspective of the client will be that of the originating planetary consciousness. From there it may or may not address the fact that other consciousness exists within the collective they originated from.

This unique difference in perspective is because the planetary consciousness created the fragment that is the client.

From the perspective of the planetary consciousness, the descriptions will depend upon what is in the best interest of the client but generally will revolve around nurturing and stewardship of the planet and life within its care. This is a result of the investment the consciousness has in the construct and the ascension of life upon it. It has existed since the formation of the material sphere and has focused its attention upon the operation of it since that moment. This may manifest as discussions of consciousness within solidified planetary matter, atmospheric gases, or the planet itself, but the view is an overall perspective and not a literal embodiment of consciousness within the inanimate object described.

GALACTIC CONSCIOUSNESS

As fully charged consciousnesses, the perspective of the cosmos from this vantage point will be one of complete understanding. There are two types of galactic-capable consciousnesses: consciousness formed within and ejected directly from God Source, and collectives that have attained this responsibility by ascending into the capability.

When the connection is established to the totality of the client's consciousness, he or she will find himself/herself at the pinnacle of creation. The pitfall to this viewpoint is that when a fragment from Earth is connected to this awareness, there are no longer any questions that need to be answered. This may result in the client's launching into a discussion fueled by an internal narrative, where the questions are asked silently by the client's fragment. The galactic consciousness then audibly provides the answers to the unheard questions. Conversely, the client may be in awe of the knowledge he or she is in contact with and remain silent as he or she basks in the feeling of knowingness. In either instance, it will take a skilled practitioner to identify what is occurring and how to proceed.

A fully ascended consciousness does not have the need to manifest an energy body. Discussions of glowing orbs and shimmering bodies will only occur if clients require these visuals to interpret what they are observing. Regardless of whether the galactic is a single organic entity or a collective composite, the view and discussion will be related from the perspective of a single consciousness. For a collective that has accepted the responsibility, this is a result of the realignment required to exist directly within the unfiltered God Source energy web, as previously discussed.

PART 3

ASSISTANCE FOR ASCENDING CONSCIOUSNESS

CHAPTER SIXTEEN

With an understanding of the construction of the cosmos, your consciousness, and your purpose within creation, we now proceed to perhaps most immediately useful portion of this book. Some of the information may appear repetitious at first, when viewed against the backdrop of extensive literature on the subjects. This book is meant to be a concise aggregate of information needed for ascending consciousness. To achieve that goal, this section contains distilled information that will assist you, devoid of flowery prose and confusing concepts.

UNDERSTANDING THE POLARITY CONSTRUCT

We contemplated omitting a detailed discussion of polarity from this book. After extensive observation, negative polarity has been found to be an inefficient construct that upsets the galactic energy balance by propagating negativity that is unable to self-reconcile. The effort required to manage and constrain it exceeds the value provided by the experiences, and if allowed to continue would have resulted in irreparable damage to the rotation and energy production of this galaxy. The eradication of this construct is in the final phases and it will soon be relegated to the dustbin of history in all space-time constructs within this galaxy. This book will exist within the transitional period on Earth as negative polarity rises to the surface to be cleared. An understanding of the construct and the events witnessed is therefore appropriate.

First, we must address the difference between the definition of polarity on Earth and the cosmic definition of polarity. We again state, for clarification, that the terms we use to define the constituent components are the closest approximations we can offer for ease of understanding.

We have discussed the nature of consciousness and that the gaining of experience in all its forms creates a charge that is stored within the photonic array. When this energy reaches a sufficient level within the array of the photons of consciousness, it creates a rotational geometry and an oscillating interaction between these photons. These two in unison produce an electromagnetic emanation because of the movement of the photons within the magnetic fields each creates. Previous concepts in this book explained that this emanation creates a barrier around the consciousness that protects the integrity of the unique energy each contains. This barrier also creates an electrical charge that is transmitted directly into the energy web of the construct in which you reside. This is the factor of conscious entropy we previously alluded to. The charge that each consciousness emanates in an amount relative to its photonic density and energy capacitance is what powers the universe. In every other galactic construct within the cosmos, there is no resistance that would oppose or negate this energy. Without interference, it is transferred through the planetary and system consciousnesses and ultimately collected by the galactic consciousness. As the creations within the galaxy become fruitful, excess energy is felt by the galactic consciousness. This excess energy begins to amass and is ultimately returned to God Source. This is the positive, unabated energy that exists throughout creation. While this discussion describes the default energy of consciousness as positive, this is only to provide clarity. Outside of this galactic construct, there is no polarity; there is only unity with the energy of the cosmos. As you exist in unity with creation, it is more appropriately considered immersion, rather than a flow of energy resulting from a potential. We want to dissolve any concepts that infer that negative polarity is required to provide balance within the galaxy or the universe. The construct of negative polarity has created the opposite result, and any ideas that espouse negativity as a necessary evil are misguided and should be discarded.

We do not want to make this book into a discussion of muons, gluons, and the helical ringlets of gravitons that comprise the space-time lattice your science understands. What we would rather state is that the entirety of the cosmos exists within the unity energy and consciousness of God Source. With this perspective, you see that everything exists within the photonic density that is understood to be the entirety of the cosmos. The discussions in this book have defined consciousness photons as spherical, spinning, and containing discreet amounts of energy. You can then deduce that every effect you observe within the cosmos, both seen and unseen, is a result of forces interacting with these constituent photons. The interaction with the constituents of God Source consciousness creates gravity, magnetism, and space-time, among other things, the most important of which is individualized consciousness.

We previously defined negative polarity as an inhibiting construct created by this galactic consciousness as a force to be overcome. The concept was that ascending consciousness would need to strive to overcome it, creating a more focused and determined collective. The construct of negative polarity employs a reverse rotational photonic spin that creates an energy within the photon that opposes the energy created from a normal rotation. The resulting effect is that when the two polarities of energy interact, the stronger of the two will absorb the energy of the other. It initially was assumed that consciousness would begin to feel uncomfortable as it accumulated negative polarity within itself. Consciousness would then reach a threshold where it would be so far removed from the energy of God Source that it would shed the negative, cease being the impediment, and return to the collective, expanded by the experience. With this explanation, you understand that the intention of the negative polarity construct was to be a moderate obstacle that positive collectives could overcome as they strive to ascend.

From an ascended viewpoint, the manifestations of negative polarity within embodied consciousness are easily recognizable because they do not align with the responses to outside stimulus that occur in a nonpolarized consciousness. A consciousness that does not contain any traces of negativity will not have self-serving interests or the submanifestations of hatred, anger, or violence as available responses. This is because the energy required to elicit these thought patterns within the consciousness does not exist. On Earth, the influences of negative polarity are so engrained that existence without them seems impossible.

Emotions are a fundamental response of the human vehicle to the external factors encountered. Everyone assumes that the spectrum of emotional responses—love, compassion, empathy, fear, anger, hatred, violence—is normal and fundamentally exists within everyone. From the perspective that they all exist, you then conclude that you must suppress the negative responses to be a better person.

Consider the responses of a baby who has not yet attained the programming of the construct. The emotions of love and compassion are noticed and felt emanating from the baby almost as soon as the child opens his or her eyes. The manifestations of anger and hatred will appear later, as the child acquires negative polarity and begins to observe these responses in others. It is easy to dismiss this as nothing more than children growing into their full range of emotions as their bodies grow and brains develop. The unseen factor, however, is the negative polarity that accumulates within the photonic consciousness of the child. With this understanding, the emotions of anger, hatred, and violence should not be viewed as inherent qualities that must be suppressed. They are learned behaviors that should be discarded along with the negative polarity that created them. From here, let's expand our discussion to the manifestations of negative polarity.

Fear

The manifestations of fear are a result of second-density instinctual behaviors that have not yet been released. Fear is a behavior programmed within all second-density organisms that assisted in their continued survival. This helped assure that they would fulfill their function within the construct. As a self-aware consciousness, the experience of fear—a lower density construct—reduces the photonic oscillations and inhibits connection to higher-order energies. For this reason, fear is meant to be released as consciousness ascends into a higher understanding. Fear is then replaced with logic and reason in higher consciousness, which performs the same function of preservation without the vibratory-reducing impact. With this explanation, you see that fear is not a direct manifestation of negative polarity. It is a response that negative consciousness attempts to elicit to assert control. To experience fear at all, we must first forget that we are inextinguishable consciousness playing in a space-time construct. From that perspective, what is there to fear?

Self-Interest

This was the initial objective of the negative-polarity construct and was expected to be the only manifestation that would then create the division that impeded collectivity. Since polarity was a new creation, the scope of what ultimately occurred could not have been anticipated. Prior to this experiment, all consciousness existing within the cosmos worked in unison and existed within the creational energy that elicits love, compassion, and empathy for everything that exists. These are the expected responses from embodied consciousness as everyone works together.

As with the first destructive tests on Earth that liberated the binding energy of creation (atomic detonations), the postulated results of the tests varied widely. The expected results were assumptions until the test was completed and the data analyzed.

During the early stages of the experiment, it appeared to be a successful creation. It impeded the creation of collectives enough that the collectives that did form were more determined and focused. As the experiment continued, the first signs of an anomaly was noticed. Rather than feeling uncomfortable as they strayed farther away from God Source energy, the negatively aligned consciousnesses became more determined and focused. As the negativity grew within consciousness, their separation from other consciousnesses grew, and new ideals that served self-interest began to manifest. Resentment for the positive collectives that were overpowering them appeared, which grew into anger and ultimately hatred. If a positive collective could form that then became a formidable force to encounter, so too could a negatively aligned collective be created that could overcome them. If the objective of negative polarity was to create self-interest, then the collectives they created would mirror this desire. The collectives formed by negative polarity contained a hierarchical power structure, where the most negative influenced and infected those below. The structure of hierarchy and segregation of power remains the most easily identifiable aspect of a negatively aligned collective.

With the understanding that the default energy of creation is positive, negative polarity was created to be easily neutralized by a larger positive polarity force. This created mixed results to negative attempts at overpowering positive collectives through energy alone. The submanifestation of hatred within the negatives created another unexpected result—violence. This was a new expression of negativity that never had been considered, and the positive collectives had no response to this new expression. With this new development, the negatives quickly gained domination over the worlds they inhabited. The immediate success of this new creation ingrained it deeply within the negative collectives, and entire planets of consciousness succumbed to negative polarity. Some of these negative planets had space-faring capabilities and began conquering unprepared positive planets that had no defense. Why would you need defenses if you were positively aligned and had no concept of self-interest or the submanifestations it creates?

HATE

This expression is unique to this galactic construct and is unknown throughout the rest of the cosmos. It manifests in various ways, but the underlying theme is division from unity in all its facets. On Earth you can find the messages of division and conflict lurking in every corner of life. This is one of the primary creations of negative polarity, whose job is to create division and discord that must be overcome as you strive for unity with each other and God Source. Reams of paper could be used to discuss the manifestations of this expression. It is far better to lay down the obsolete and allow it to slowly fade from view.

ANGER/VIOLENCE

Another expression that is only found in this galaxy and is a submanifestation of hate. When the construct of negative polarity was created, it was not anticipated that it would create the desire within consciousness to inflict damage or end the embodiment of another consciousness against its will. When this result was first observed, it was not completely understood what mechanisms had created this unforeseen desire within consciousness. As with any experiment where unanticipated results are obtained, it was observed and allowed to continue so it could be understood.

Two aspects of negative polarity are the most important to understand and will assist in its dissolution:

- It is easily transferable between consciousnesses.
- It is easily neutralized by positive polarity (God Source/unity energy).

AVOIDING/REALIGNING NEGATIVE POLARITY

Avoiding and removing negative polarity would appear to be a daunting task as you witness the events occurring on Earth during the time this book was published. If you follow news reports, it appears that negativity is hiding in every corner or not hiding at all. The reality, of course, is much simpler; you are deliberately shown things that are biased toward the negative. Contrary to what some might believe, this is not a statement that illuminates the nefarious intentions of negative entities that attempt to control you. You are shown what the majority has wanted to hear, and the media gives you what they think you want. This perception is driven by the viewer ratings that are obtained as various content is offered. If the ratings of these programs suddenly plummeted because no one was interested in watching them, the content would change. As previously stated, until recently the polarities on Earth have been skewed toward the negative. This has resulted in the acceptance of manifestations of negativity as normal and has created a dulling of consciousness to the effects imparted through the experience of negativity.

If every night you turn on the same news channel and listen to the narrative presented, at some point in this repetitive action, the narrative effects a change within your consciousness. That change will depend on the individuals and the rotational balance within their consciousnesses that exists beyond the veil. Let us consider some possible results to viewing negatively biased information, the current major component of the news agencies.

- Do you turn on the news and look in horror at the images presented?
- Does the narrative create anger or hatred in you as you stand on one side or the other of the division created?
- Do the stories create fear within you as you fixate on the worst possible outcome?
- Do the images of the rich and entitled create a feeling of lack or resentment within you as you struggle with self-serving desires?

If you experience these obviously negative responses and still turn on the same program each night, you should question the reasoning behind that behavior. The responses everyone expresses without thinking associated with negative polarity are habitual. You have been doing the same thing for so long that you unconsciously respond to outside stimulus. As consciousnesses continue to shed negativity, they will reach a threshold where they will become sensitive to the effects and responses of negative polarity. Once you can identify a thing, you can avoid it. When you consciously monitor your reactions to outside factors, you can dissolve and realign your responses.

As mentioned, negative polarity within consciousness manifests as self-interest, division, hatred, anger, and violence. A multitude of nuances are associated with these core manifestations, and as you shed negativity, they will become self-evident. The most important aspect of these is that they can be discarded as responses and avoided altogether. Before you can effectively avoid negative polarity, you must first understand how easily it is transferred between consciousnesses.

ACQUIRING NEGATIVE POLARITY

Consider that there are two individual third-density consciousnesses that are about to be within proximity of each other. One is generally positive and exists within an energy of love and kindness. The other consciousness is negatively charged due to the experiences it has attracted. Neither has an awareness of the constituents of consciousness, but for this example, consider that the negatively aligned consciousness contains a higher order of polarization due to repetitive experiences of negativity. The two now find their barrier membranes within proximity of each other as they sit in a waiting room. The positive consciousness initially sat down with a generally happy demeanor but with no knowledge of polarity or the constituents of consciousness. In their ignorance, they allow energy transference through their respective membranes.

Since the negatively aligned consciousness is of a greater magnitude, it will affect the energy signature of the positive consciousness. The observable effect will be that the mood of the positive individual slowly changes as the higher order energy realigns the other. For example, the positive individual may have arrived in no hurry, with the expectation he or she would wait if required. As the realignment occurs, however, his or her mood begins to shift. The individual now watches the hands of the clock, and as the realignment continues, he or she becomes increasingly irritated. The positive consciousness has been negatively polarized without recognizing what occurred or why its mood suddenly changed.

The above example occurs millions of times each day as you find yourselves within proximity of one another. While the example was of a higher-order negative realigning positivity, the reverse also is true. Consciousness with an abundance of positive polarity can walk through a room and realign the negativity that exists there. We prefer this example to the first and suggest that everyone exist within a space of overpowering positive polarity. A positive polarity easily will realign a negatively infected consciousness if the positive entity understands the mechanics of consciousness. If a positively aligned consciousness knows to hold its space and how to reject negativity effectively, the negative polarity could be of a greater magnitude and still be overpowered and dissipated. Negatively aligned consciousness understands this at an instinctual level. This manifests as an uncomfortable feeling in the entity when it is in the presence of an overpowering polarity. Because of that, negatively aligned consciousnesses will physically avoid a consciousness that they know can overpower them.

If you are an ascending consciousness, you probably can think of more than one occasion when someone was within your proximity and quickly found a reason to depart. Unless you have questionable hygiene habits, this is probably the reason it occurred. As you would expect, this also works in the opposite direction. Have you ever met someone that you know nothing about and has done nothing to you, yet you feel like that person is dragging you down just by being in his or her presence? If you have, we must congratulate you. That is the sensory response of an ascending consciousness beginning to feel the drain of negative polarity upon its energy. As you continue to work in consciousness and embrace the techniques discussed in this book and others, you will feel the drain less often. As the positivity continues to increase within you, negativity will avoid you altogether, and your life will change.

THE END OF NEGATIVE POLARITY

The ending of the polarity experiment within this galaxy has been underway for a long period of time-space. The manifestations of violence and conquest were unexpected by-products that initially caught the positively aligned collectives off guard. When the call went out for assistance in ending the experiment without compromising the balance of the galaxy, the solution was a paradox. To remove the infection without destroying the galaxy, the positive collectives would have to embrace the methods of negative polarity. Violence and conquest require the ending of embodiment against the will of the consciousness. Until the decision was made to combat the infection with its own creations, this was unheard of in positive collectives. Positive collectives throughout the cosmos had no understanding or experience with violence or warfare. The weapons, tactics, and battle strategies required did not exist beyond the observations of positive consciousnesses that had been the recipients of such actions. Since you cannot force a disembodied consciousness to cooperate if it does not want to, the acquisition of this knowledge would require a different approach. The answer to this dilemma was to find disembodied consciousnesses with these experiences whose polarity still allowed them to connect to positive collectives. Ascended consciousness would be sent to collectives that contained this experience and attempt to recruit the best prospects. As disembodied consciousness, you know the objective is to collect experience, and this would be like no other.

As the response began, entire planets of completely negative embodied consciousnesses were eradicated, regardless of the timeline within which they existed. This halted the expansion of the infection in the physical. This also allowed the disembodied negative consciousnesses affected by the conflict to be realigned. As their incarnations were forcibly ended, they were denied access to their etheric collectives and redirected to the creational interface at the center of the galactic consciousness. Through a slow and controlled process that allowed the galactic to maintain its energy balance, correcting the negative polarity imbalance had begun.

Since the actions of violence and killing create negativity within consciousness, elaborate steps were taken to ensure positive consciousnesses engaged in these actions were not lost to the polarities to which they were exposed. The consciousness of the volunteers was monitored, and as threshold burdens of negativity accrued, they would need to be cleared of the infection. Positive polarity portals were created, which consciousness would then enter. Within them, the negative polarities acquired during the eradications were overpowered and dissipated within the perceived white light of creational energy. This is a carefully controlled process because if the energy required to remove the negativity is too great, the entire experience of the consciousness can be lost as it is completely realigned. Due to the conceptualization of light flooding the consciousness that is experienced during clearing and the glowing enclosures that are entered, these portals were affectionately dubbed; *light chambers*.

All levels of ascended consciousness have been engaged in ending this experiment. The knowledge and technology of the universe has been brought to bear to remove this infection.

All of this has occurred in multiple offsetting quadrants of this galaxy, where completely negative systems and planets existed. Earth, while struggling with negative polarity for a long time, has not been completely overrun. This is due in part to the selfless actions of several ascended consciousnesses who volunteered to come here and bring ascended teachings. These individuals are easy to spot if you look back upon the history of this timeline. Some even have religions that sprang up around their teachings. While these teachings did not survive intact, they provided enough insight and direction to slow the spread of negativity.

In looking at the current situation on Earth, it might appear as if the world is getting worse instead of better. We assure you that is not the case. What you are witnessing is negativity rising to the surface in consciousness so that it may be cleared. We acknowledge that there still is a small percentage of negatively aligned consciousnesses who are pushing their agendas. What they notice, however, is that their actions no longer have the same effect they once had on consciousness. Larger expressions of negative polarity produce smaller results because the polarities have shifted. Like a person trapped in a compartment filling with water, they are looking for whatever pocket of air they can find to continue their existence. They know it is futile and that realignment is approaching if they are completely negative and cannot turn into the light of unity. Despite the inevitability of the outcome, they will cling to the last moments of existence until there is no air left, and they take the last breath.

The balance of positive and negative polarity within this galaxy is rapidly reaching an acceptable level. At that point, the power required for the unity wave to eradicate negativity will be low enough that it will not impact the energy of experience in positive consciousness. When this threshold is reached, the wave will commence. Positive consciousness will feel this wave as an immersion in a pool of absolute bliss. As the wave passes, all traces of negativity and its sub-manifestations will cease forever. You then will look back upon your history, puzzled by the actions of your ancestors. The events will have been colored by the darkness of polarity, and you no longer will have any concept of anything beyond unity consciousness.

CHAPTER SEVENTEEN
LOVE FOR SELF, LOVE FOR ALL

This section will use the terms and concepts you commonly associate with the frequency and wavelength of God Source energy. We will not include any discussions of heavily infected negative-polarity consciousness. As we have indicated, negatively aligned consciousness will avoid positive polarity or consider it a threat and eliminate it. In this section, our discussions will be of consciousness that is positive or that has not yet exceeded the threshold of negativity that prevents it from turning and once again immersing itself in creational energy to be cleansed.

The ascended consciousnesses who came here to assist in the past were limited in their ability to properly define the concepts. The limitation was not based on their understandings, but by the teachings that could be assimilated by the consciousness that existed during the time of their incarnations. Discussions of spinning photons, energy signatures, and toroidal spheres would have been met with blank stares. As previously stated, the message is tailored to the level the consciousness can accept. Many examples of paintings and drawings of these ascended beings still exist and can be used to identify what the people of that era saw and experienced. It is not a coincidence that pictures of these teachers portray them with golden auras around them, emanating from them, or stylized as halos above their heads. There are also paintings of your deities with their hearts visible outside of their bodies, radiating shimmering golden rays in all directions. Some may observe these obviously noncorporeal representations and consider them the trappings of religious dogma, where the entity who is the focus of the religion is idolized and elevated to solicit worship. From our perspective, we understand these representations are misidentified conceptualizations of what the masses observed and experienced.

The vibration and frequency of love is a tangible commodity that can be felt when you are within proximity of it. When a consciousness understands this frequency and has the capability to harness it within its rotating geometry, anyone in the same proximity will feel the effects and know there is something different about that person. The frequency associated with love is the default energy of creation in which all consciousness instinctually feels at home. During the time these ascended consciousnesses incarnated, the polarities were heavily negative.

Imagine being a consciousness that has wandered blindly upon Earth within the darkness of negative polarity. At the photonic level of your consciousness, you know what the frequency of positive creational energy feels like because you were created from it. Now there is a person on the planet with ascended knowledge who has cleared his or her consciousness of negativity through concentrated effort and is teaching this knowledge to others. Having read this far in the book, you know that because of the overwhelming positivity this person contains, consciousnesses in proximity will feel the effects of being cleansed of negative polarity. As the negativity dissipates and the energy increases within the consciousness, they begin to feel the seat of consciousness (heart center) awaken and energize. Having never felt this before and not knowing what is occurring, they will not want to leave the side of this unique entity. If the ascended consciousness was provided additional density for its mission, it may also be able to manipulate, bend, or break the rules of the governing construct.

The purpose of these ascended incarnations was to drop a beacon of light into the ocean of darkness that was Earth at the time. This allowed those not lost to the polarities the ability to set their courses using this beacon and find their way out of the darkness. As with any teaching, as students grow, the lessons must grow with them.

Defining Love

The current perceptions of love on Earth fall into categories where various flavors of the perceived emotion are then experienced. You "fall" in love with someone based upon the predefined parameters that you think the object of your affection should contain. You love your parents in a different manner than you love your partner, which is different than the love you feel for your friends. These gradients of love are a result of associating emotional responses with a misunderstanding of what creates the expansion within the heart center (seat of consciousness).

When you begin your search for a partner to love, you usually begin with a checklist of characteristics your partner should have. The idea of the perfect partner is shaped by the environment within which your ego construct is programmed. Among the various cultures, you will find differing templates of the ideal partner that you then fall in love with and, if all goes well, produce offspring and live your lives together. For this reason, one culture may not understand the templates of another, yet the ideal of love is accepted as the thread that sews them all together.

Every living thing is consciousness, created from and existing within the consciousness of the cosmos. Creational energy is transmitted from the seat of the cosmic consciousness and exists uniformly from one end of the universe to the other. As you absorb this energy and draw it into your body, you exist in unity with the energy of creation. A connection to this energy is a connection to your creator, and every particle of your construction instinctively knows this. Existing in separation on Earth has disconnected you from this energy. Therefore, whenever you reconnect to this energy during embodiment, even briefly, you instinctively want to grasp it and try to remain in the energy any way possible.

CHAKRAS/ENERGY NODES

There is no shortage of literature discussing the chakras of the human vehicle. This book will not repeat them, but some discussion is required so that their relationship to the concepts presented here are understood. The energy flow within the body and through the chakras is in both directions. Our focus for this section will be on the effects this energy system plays to elicit the experiences associated with love in the body and within consciousness.

In a previous chapter, we said that Earth contains an energy grid with nodes that allow the proper sequencing and overlay of spacetime constructs. These energy nodes are used by the planetary consciousness, and from there you can loosely infer that the crust and mantle components of Earth are the body of this consciousness. The human vehicle also is an energy system powered by consciousness. At 100 percent efficiency, the energy of consciousness would be enough to completely sustain the body. You are currently, in automotive terms, a hybrid, in the fact that the energy needs of your body are supplemented by the conversion of matter into energy through digestion. As ascension continues, this requirement will fall away as you obtain more energy from consciousness and less from digestion. This will occur naturally under the pressure of increasing conscious energy and cannot be forced, so do not decide to stop eating tomorrow because you read this. You may decide, however, to eat more appropriately, and this will be discussed shortly.

To power your body and to receive feedback from it, the energy of consciousness has been tethered to the body at discreet energy node points that are known as chakras. For ease of understanding, consider that these energy points provide increasing voltages to the body. The switch to each of them is turned on through the increasing density, balance, and rotation of the toroidal sphere of consciousness. More power and balance in your consciousness equates directly to the switches being thrown and more power being provided to your body. As these chakras provide power to the body, they also provide increased awareness related to their activation and operation. They are activated from the base upward but also have a direct connection to your consciousness. When all are activated and aligned, creational energy then flows from the top downward, empowering the body. With this basic understanding, we turn our attention to the three chakras that have a direct effect on the sensation and interpretation of the creational energy associated with love.

Root Chakra

Root chakra is the base energy node that is activated in second density. It is associated with the instinctual behaviors that ensure survival and procreation. As the toroidal sphere attains third-density geometry and enters the human form, this is the initial chakra from which the consciousness operates. As the lessons accumulate and the consciousness grows, the successive chakras are meant to be activated. As they activate, the observed perception of the embodied consciousness is also expected to activate and ascend beyond the instinctual.

Physical attraction is a programmed instinctual behavior. In birds, the colorful feathers attract a partner based upon the perception that a healthy plume equates to a healthy mate with which to procreate. This ensures the continuation of the species through the proper sequencing of genetic material. Selection based upon outward appearance carries into the human vehicle for use in the primitive timelines and is meant to be released as the consciousness continues to evolve. In the complex societies you currently exist in, choosing a partner based solely upon responses initiated by the root chakra will prove unsuccessful or strained. The evidence of this is pervasive and needs no further illumination. The frequencies of love are not felt in the root/base chakra; existing solely in this chakra allows the manifestations of negative polarity to become outwardly apparent. Activating the higher chakras moderates the lower chakras and increases the energy available as it begins to flow in the proper direction.

Heart Chakra

Prior to the complete activation of this energy node, you will feel the base chakra pushing energy into this chakra as it responds to the stimulus of instinctual/conditioned behaviors. When triggered, the root chakra overflows with energy, and it flows upward into the heart chakra. While activated from the wrong direction, the heart chakra responds, and the perception is a feeling of being in love with the object causing the activation. The energy sent to the heart chakra from the root is a trickle compared to what occurs from the other direction. While low, the energy is still enough to cause the heart chakra to energize and connect to God Source energy. The magnitude of God Source energy accessed will depend on how much energy is produced by the root chakra. This energy will not last, and the heart activation will fade as the energy from the root chakra subsides.

As consciousness gains balance, additional energy becomes available as subsequent chakras/energy nodes align and provide their energy and stability to the body. When the heart chakra aligns, and the energy is felt coursing through the body for the first time, the feeling will elicit the desire to simultaneously laugh and cry in joy. As the heart center opens to the energies of creation, the physical sensation could be compared to the sun shining from within. A heart center activation can occur through concerted effort by the consciousness, or it could be activated through being in proximity to a fully aligned consciousness. In the second instance, the overwhelming positive polarity of the aligned consciousness is realigning photonic spin and removes negativity in the unawakened as the toroidal spheres overlap. An activation in this manner will completely open the heart chakra, and the effects will be unlike anything experienced. The energy of the heart chakra is usually associated with romantic love, and this can cause confusion if the mechanics of what occurs is not understood. The ascended consciousnesses that walked the earth performed this service to all they interacted with and left teachings to be practiced that would continue their work.

When the heart chakra opens and begins to provide energy into the body, the rotational balance and positivity of the consciousness has reached a threshold where the existence of negative polarity can be felt as a foreign object and dissipated. These outward emotional expressions of negativity are associated with ingrained habits that have not yet been discarded but are now observed from a higher perspective. With this new awareness, the manifestations of negativity that still exist within the consciousness can be cleared internally through intention. The proper operation of this energy node is an important step along the path toward immersion in the unity of creational energy. This energy center, sitting above the root chakra—and those in between—pushes positive energy downward and into the lower energy centers. When the base chakra becomes energized by creational energy, the instinctual behaviors subside and are no longer the driver of action within the ego construct. This is a critical step in ascension because the heart chakra then pushes this energy upward into the crown chakra, and the final awakening commences.

To understand the importance of the heart chakra/energy node, we must revisit the repeating nature of the construction of consciousness. Recall that the toroidal sphere of consciousness has whirlpools at the top and bottom that meet in the middle. At the center of this column is the seat of consciousness, which is the interface between the creational energy of the cosmos and material creations of matter. While embodied, your perspective of consciousness is behind your eyes, and you associate that with your brain. The reality is that your heart center is the actual seat of your consciousness. If you overlay the whirlpool column of consciousness upon the image of the chakra energy system, you will see that the energy of consciousness has two pathways to flow into the chakra system from the heart and empower the body.

If the energy is flowing upward in this column through the root chakra, the instinctual behaviors are highly energized and exert control over the body and the ego programming. This is the default setting that all third-density humans begin their incarnations with. This is also the energy pathway of negative polarity. The higher pathways of energy associated with ascension cannot be activated by negative energy. The higher energy nodes align the body to the frequencies of creational energy as they align the consciousness. The higher frequencies and chakras manifest thoughts and actions associated with positive polarity—unity, love, empathy, and service to the collective. Conversely, the default energy pathway, the root chakra is further energized by the dense energy of negativity as it accumulates in the consciousness, and the baser instinctual responses become the driver of manifestation. This is how negative polarity enters the body and causes responses. With this understanding, you can identify what occurs and choose to stop it. We will now return to the discussion of energy pathways and disregard any further negative polarity influences.

As you acquire the proper energy of experience and rotational balance, the flow of energy reverses through your energy conduit. The previous discussions of creating galaxies and systems of planets all centered upon the use of creational energy flowing from the seat of the respective consciousnesses. As you identify your heart chakra as the seat of your consciousness and the interface to creational energy, you will understand the importance of its proper operation. With this energy node activated, creational energy comes directly into the column and flows in both directions. This energy flow balances and moderates the lower chakras and awakens the higher chakras. It is not a coincidence that creational energy through the heart center is required for the continued awakening and empowerment of embodied consciousness. As stated, love, compassion, and empathy are requirements to access higher order abilities.

CROWN CHAKRA

There is more than one reason this energy node has been identified as the crown. This is the final chakra that, when activated, allows the influx of conscious energy and knowledge into the body and inside the veil of forgetfulness. When a fully aligned energy stream is observed by sensitives, it appears as a colorful vortex above the head as the energy flows into the focal point at the top of the whirlpool column of the toroidal sphere. How far above the physical body this crown will appear is a function of how much energy exists within the consciousness sphere. A consciousness containing excessive density and energy will have a toroidal membrane that extends far beyond the physical form. In this instance, the focal point of the energy will enter the top of the column far above the head and may be misunderstood as an additional chakra.

With the heart chakra activated, positive energy now flows up through the column, and the crown chakra alignment commences. The time required for alignment and opening is dependent upon the individual and the focus of his or her consciousness. If the consciousness was actively seeking enlightenment and deliberately opened the heart chakra, the opening of the crown will be accelerated. This is because the physical feedback, sensed when the heart opened, is not unexpected but is embraced. This reinforces the desire of the individual to continue along his or her path with increased determination. If the heart opened unexpectedly due to a realignment that occurred in proximity to an ascended consciousness, a period of understanding what occurred and why is needed, and a slow opening of the crown will provide this direction.

An open crown chakra allows a complete connection to the toroidal consciousness and the energy and knowledge associated with it. Returning to the repeating nature of consciousness, we observe the same toroidal architecture in God Source, galactic, system, and planetary consciousness. These consciousnesses exist within higher-order consciousness and draw the energy for their creations from the photonic energy web of the consciousness they exist within. They obviously do not digest matter; they obtain all the energy they need through immersion. With this understanding, it becomes clear that the toroidal sphere of individual consciousness also has this ability. It is currently tethered to vehicles that require digestion, but creational energy is still available for the expansion of the energy systems of the body and increasing the density of consciousness when a clear connection has been established.

With the crown open, higher-order intelligence begins to assert control within the consciousness. The perspective is one of acceptance and collectivity as the constructs of separation created through the lower chakra and negative polarity become transparent. The view is one from the top of a mountain, and the path leading to the summit is clearly visible. Looking back upon the road traveled, the obstacles that seemed so difficult when encountered now appear obvious and childish. As the exhilaration of reaching the summit begins to subside, you become aware of the crowd that stands there with you. The conversations and thoughts you share on the mountaintop will not resemble the conversations that occur in the valley. Again, there is no judgment in this statement; those at the summit will welcome everyone as their journey leads them there. The reality of standing at this summit is that as you turn from the accomplishment of ascending from the valley, you see that the path forward leads to the next mountain.

Colorful metaphors aside, the crown chakra is the gateway that, when opened, allows an unhindered flow of creational energy into the toroidal whirlpool column. A connection to this energy performs several higher-order functions:

- As creational energy flows through the chakras, any remaining misalignments are resolved. The human vehicle is designed to take advantage of energy that arrives through the chakras, and if/when it becomes available, the body will respond. With the proper intention of consciousness, this energy can then be used to heal injury and slow the effects of aging.

- A connection to higher intelligence becomes available, which begins to provide answers to the questions of consciousness. When coupled with the resulting feelings of love, compassion, and empathy, this will manifest as a desire to share knowledge and assist others.

- With concentrated effort, the flow of energy from your consciousness can be used to connect to the sensory capabilities of your toroidal sphere. This allows the viewing of auras, sensing the intentions of others, telepathy, and the remaining laundry list of mystical arts. What manifests will depend upon the individual and the density, energy, and balance within their toroidal spheres.

As the new knowledge and awareness settles into the consciousness, a complete understanding materializes. Love is no longer seen as a response to an external object; it is understood to be a frequency of energy that exists within and is shared unconditionally with others. The connection to your toroidal sphere allows additional sensory capabilities that were previously unknown. You will feel things about others because of the interaction of auras when in proximity with you. It is here that the identification of the twin flame/duality aspect occurs. Since you are literally cut from the same cloth, the sympathetic resonant action of your entwining energies will be unmistakable. The amplification of your energies will be felt in your respective heart chakras as they overflow and purge any misalignments from your body. When this milestone has been reached, you will be at the last lesson of third density for an organically ascending consciousness.

HOLDING THE FREQUENCY OF LOVE

This sounds like a simple task—to just walk around in the frequency of creational energy. Why would that be difficult? With all your chakras open, the energy should just pour out of you anyway. In a nonpolarity world, this is exactly what happens because there is no impediment to unity or anything that would negate the positivity of creational energy. Unfortunately, Earth exists within the galaxy that created polarity. With the energies of negativity waning, it is more important than ever to awaken all who are ready and align them to the frequencies of love so that unity is accelerated, and division is abolished forever. To that end, you must understand how to hold the frequencies of love against consciousnesses that carry negativity. Regardless of whether they are aware of their burden, the negativity they carry will attempt to reduce your positivity if you allow it.

We previously described an interaction between a negatively charged consciousness and a positively charged one. During this interaction, the positive person noticed his mood changed as the polarity shifted within him. While the example was one of a slow change in perspective and mood, the amount of change and the rate at which it occurs will depend upon the magnitude of the differential between the two consciousnesses. This is an electromagnetic exchange of energy, and it operates under the same principles as electrical circuits—the greater the electrical potential between the conductors, the faster the transfer occurs. Since this is a transfer of electrical potential, it follows that the potential between the two conductors can be lessened or interrupted by using an insulator. Since we are discussing consciousness and an exchange of energy outside of the material, the construction of the insulator must also consist of an unseen component.

Self-aware consciousness is a toroidal sphere of energized photons that oscillate and create an electromagnetic barrier that extends beyond the rotating sphere. As previously mentioned, this barrier membrane protects the integrity of the energy of experience contained within it. The permeability of this membrane can be manipulated through the focus of conscious intention. Consciousnesses with no knowledge of this membrane or the interactions of polarity that occur, walk around with this membrane wide open. As they walk through a crowd, they unknowingly attract and disburse energy through whatever potentials exist between the consciousnesses they are in proximity with. No insulation to these energies has been erected, and they transfer unabated.

Consider the demonstrations that occur around the world and some of the violence that results from them. When viewed on the television from the safety of your home, you might not understand why the tensions continue to rise, and the crowd reacts with violence. Outside of the influence of the polarities, the behavior appears irrational, but to those immersed in the protest, the story is different. We have termed negative polarity as an infection, and that is exactly what occurs—consciousness in proximity is infected with the polarities as the electrical potential causes the transfer. Imagine that the demonstration we are discussing is instead a swarm of angry bees near a hive. The bees are mad at something, and a small swarm becomes a larger one as bees that were collecting pollen away from the hive see the swarm and join it. These bees do not know why the others are angry, only that it must be justified because they are bees from the same hive. Now there is a huge swarm of angry bees, even though most of them have no idea why they are angry or where to focus their attack. Since the construct of negative polarity is one of self-interest and hierarchy, at the center of any swarm there will be a few bees who have instigated and are controlling what occurs. The magnitude of negativity at the center of the swarm radiates outward and affects everyone. The negativity is not insulated, and as it spreads, it amplifies through the feedback of additional conscious intention. If left to spread uncontrolled, the negativity eventually will reach a threshold where it manifests as physical responses.

A single entity attempting to hold a frequency of love in proximity with negative polarity of this magnitude would require a consciousness experienced in manipulating its energetic membrane and concentrated effort. However, a group of positively aligned entities who have focused their intent upon dissipating the negativity in the crowd would have far more success. The techniques for manipulating your energetic membrane are provided in Part 4.

Sharing the Frequency of Love

As we have discussed, sharing your frequency is an automatic process that occurs through the electrical potential that exists between consciousnesses. It is then correct to assume that a completely positive consciousness can walk among others and realign everyone in its proximity. If it remains the overpowering polarity, it will not feel the drain associated with any negativity it encounters and subsequently dissipates. The important aspect is that it remains the overpowering polarity that absorbs the negative charge without a reduction in intensity. It may observe the outward manifestations of negativity within others, but like a kitchen cleanser, it will disinfect all it touches. The impacted consciousness may never be able to identify when a change occurred, but the realignment has shifted the energy and photonic spin of the sphere. In time, it will notice a change in its outlook and behavior as the predilection toward negative responses subsides.

Consciousness becomes accustomed to the existence of negative polarity within it and the emotional responses it creates. Like driving the same road to work every day, these habitual responses to outside stimulus are hardly noticed. It is used to the burden it is carrying and does not notice it—until the weight of it has been removed. As the energy of its consciousness rebalances and resumes a positive rotation, it realigns to the energy of creation. The process of realigning the root chakra and directing energy toward the opening of the heart chakra has begun. This reduces the physical manifestations of negativity, and as the consciousness emerges from the darkness, the awakening commences. Conscious intention can increase the effectiveness of realignment and how to perform this will be discussed in Part 4.

Pets

There is another aspect of sharing the creational energy associated with love that occurs unrelated to the polarity discussion. Throughout the cosmos, a nurturing occurs as higher-order consciousness guides lower-order consciousness toward the knowledge and lessons required for ascension. This exchange involves the unity energy of God Source and is done with the same loving frequency that exists when a parent nurtures a child. This sharing of knowledge and energy occurs throughout all levels of ascending consciousness. The higher the awareness of the consciousness, the more focused the sharing becomes as the operation of consciousness within the cosmos is understood. The sharing of creational energy in all its forms and expressions causes this energy transfer to occur. The energy impacts and enriches the lower-order consciousness while in proximity to the frequencies of love by causing division to occur in the photons that contain threshold energies. As previously stated, increasing photonic density increases the ability to store energy. The photonic energy then interacts to create rotations and geometry within the conscious sphere. This is ascension.

As embodied consciousness under the veil, you are performing the service with no concept of why you are doing it, other than to give and receive the frequencies of love with a lower-density creation. On a planetary scale, you are nurturing second-density embodied consciousness and assisting its ascension into third density. The second density "pets," in all their forms, that you care for and nurture receive far more than food and shelter from your actions. The love that you feel and share with these creatures helps them in their ascension. As you consciously focus your intentions of love upon the second-density creations within your care, you expand their photonic array. You have also brought them into your homes and taught them how to interact within the human construct. The benefits are shared within your consciousness as well because selfless actions create a harmonic ringing within the conscious sphere that assists alignment. This is the reciprocity of love that all feel and instinctively desire.

As you shower these creatures with your love and affection, be mindful of the service you provide them and you. Their departure from your life at the end of their incarnations should then be considered a possible graduation. The time you shared together may have been all that was needed to propel them into third density.

Karma and Sin

We began this section with the title "Love for Self, Love for All" and would now like to focus upon the love we share internally as it relates to the concepts of karma and sin. These constructs evolved over time as the dilution of ascended teachings occurred and separate concepts were blended together through the generations.

The concept of karma is summarized as an action created in consciousness that will draw a similar reaction to that consciousness to provide balance. The original intent of karma was to explain the interactions of polarity and rotational balance to consciousness that did not have the ability to understand toroidal spheres and electromagnetic interactions. Since there is good karma and bad karma, the bad is often used as a tool of retribution and wielded against those who have committed perceived violations, using the saying, "Karma is a bitch." This has occurred because of the blending of the concept of karma with the idea of sin and its differing interpretations. These ideals have created a host of misconceptions within consciousness that then hinder it through barriers it creates for itself. If you are reading this book and understand what has been discussed, karma and sin are concepts that you have outgrown and should now release. Consider the following substitutions:

- You choose the lessons you learn in each lifetime. It is up to you to use your rotational balance to navigate to them under the veil of forgetfulness.
- Negative polarity and its manifestations are obstacles in your path that, when properly understood and identified, can be avoided and neutralized.

Positive polarity is energy in unity with God Source. Concentrated focus on drawing this energy into your photonic array will dissipate any negativity, align your energy nodes (chakras), and set you along your path to ascension.

The first step along the road to ascension is to forgive yourself for any perceived transgressions. There is no deity to beg for this reward. There is only you and the reality you are creating for yourself within a cosmos that gives you what you ask for. You must discard any belief that you are unworthy because before you can realign others with positive polarity, you first must realign yourself. As previously stated, positive polarity contains that which exists in unity with God Source. As you draw this energy into yourself, the obstacles to it will fall away as you allow and release.

This is love given to the self, which is then the love that is given to all.

CHAPTER EIGHTEEN

THE HUMAN VEHICLE

The vehicle that your consciousness is operating is a highly complex biological machine that has been designed to evolve with your consciousness. As with any machine, if you do not read the instruction manual, you will not understand how to operate it or what it is capable of. This is another topic where extensive literature exists, scattered throughout time. Since the ascension from third density to fourth density will occur for most of you during embodiment, it is prudent to include instructions that will assist the process. The following sections are the most important aspects to consider in relation to an ascending consciousness that needs its body to evolve with it.

There is more to your body than the material parts that can be dissected. Your consciousness is unseen energy that provides power to your body like a battery. For this to occur, there must be a network in place that transmits the energy throughout the body so it can be used. The brain is connected to the rest of the body through the nervous system so information about the status of the body can be interpreted. Your consciousness is then connected to the brain, which is the computer that interfaces with it and the material plane. If you impair your brain through drugs, alcohol, or trauma, you also will impair what consciousness interprets through it.

It is well known that Chinese medicine has mapped an intricate energy network that exists within the body that they use in the art of acupuncture. The principle of acupuncture is to short circuit and redirect the flow of conscious energy through the body to assist in healing and pain management. This is the circuit of the body that is designed to accept and distribute the creational energy that consciousness provides. Whether your consciousness provides a trickle or a torrent depends upon the alignment of your energy nodes (chakras) and your understanding of the dynamics of the cosmos. The ascension into fourth density during embodiment requires that you understand and energize this secondary nourishment system. As your consciousness continues to increase in energy, this system will become the dominant source of energy, and the desire to consume and digest matter will naturally fade as the human vehicle continues to evolve.

KEEP IT MOVING:
THE VALUE OF EXERCISE VS. THE COST OF INACTIVITY

The body you inhabit operates on the principle of pumping and was designed to be in motion. The systems that comprise the body require movement to perform their functions. Your body was not designed to be inactive for long periods during its lifespan. The instinctual programming of the body is conservation of energy to allow for survival during times of food scarcity. Because of this, the body instinctually stores calories not immediately needed as fat. It also reduces the caloric requirements of unneeded muscle density by reducing them when they are not being used. If you are consuming more food than required and not moving, the resulting changes in your body may not be to your liking. This instinctual programming is meant to be understood and compensated for as your consciousness ascends.

The processing and elimination of unusable material through your digestive tract is enhanced as the movement of the body helps push the material through. Without adequate movement, the material will remain in the intestines longer. Couple this increased exposure with the toxins that exist in many foods today, and disorders will result. The circulatory system also must be cycled for it to operate efficiently to provide nourishment and remove impurities from the blood and organs. Elevating your heart rate by deliberately moving the body acts to flush the impurities from the vessels and organs and transports them to the filters that will eliminate them.

Your brain is the computer interface between your consciousness and the material plane. It is the consciousness interface with your body and, along with your heart, is a critical component needed for ascension. The vessels that nourish and oxygenate this organ rely on a varying flow and pressure of blood for them to properly perform their function. The increased blood flow and pressure associated with physical activity flexes the vessel walls, helps the brain remove impurities, and increases the flow of oxygen. The most important aspect of increasing blood flow is to increase the circulation of nutrients acquired from the food you consume. This makes your nutritional selections the first important decision.

Nourishing the Body: You Are What You Eat

The first incarnation in the human vehicle is in a primitive timeline, where you become acclimated to the abilities and limitations. Consider how the requirement to nourish the body properly is learned when there is no one else to show you what to eat. Instinctual behaviors are programmed into the human as they are in the second-density life-forms to help you survive. For example, if the smell or taste of something is considered unpleasant, you will not be inclined to eat it. By the same measure, if something smells or tastes wonderful, you will be inclined to eat more of it. In these earlier times, foraging and movement is the requirement for survival. Because of this, the human is predisposed to desire foods high in calories and carbohydrates. When more calories are consumed than are required, the body is programmed to store the excess in anticipation of times when nourishment is not available. While these instinctual desires still exist, you have manipulated your construct beyond its need.

As consciousness evolves, it is expected to discard instinctual programming and replace it with logic and reason in the same manner as the instinctual response of fear. There is a distinct difference between eating to live and living to eat, and it should be obvious. The genetic predisposition of your lineage may have an impact on your body's desire and ability to store unused calories, but your consciousness is ultimately in charge. Whether you use it to take control of your body and its desires or remain at the mercy of them is your decision to make. Ascending consciousness is expected to understand what occurs and assume control over the instinctual urges.

An Unhappy Cow Makes for a Depressing Dinner

Apart from water for hydration, everything that you consume to nourish your body has at one point been alive ... or at least it should have been. This points to the fact that you are not only consuming the observable matter of that organism but also the prana, or life force, the organism imbued upon the matter it created during its existence. For a consciousness that has not opened the gateway and energy nodes within itself, the ingested prana is all that it receives. The second-density organisms that currently are cultivated for the nutritional value of their flesh have been reduced to a commodity with a value attached. To maximize the profit, large farms have been created that bear no resemblance whatsoever to the environment these creatures were designed to inhabit. From a human perspective, these animals appear to have no concept of existence beyond the instinctual behaviors that they exhibit. As we have said, consciousness is responsible for the manifestations of matter that exist within them. The animals you raise in these farms manifest the bodies that you then consume. The environment in which they live their existences is translated to their bodies through their consciousness. It is therefore prudent to have some knowledge of how the animals were raised before you consume their remains.

EAT WITH THE DIRT IN VIEW

The products that are mass produced to nourish you bear little resemblance to the food your body was designed to consume. Processed, preserved, and frozen, they are convenient packages that require little thought as they are tossed into a machine to reheat them. The machine then bombards them with electromagnetic waves that excite the molecules until they are at the desired temperature. The actual life-rejuvenating nourishment that your body receives from these products is minimal. Could any prana survive the path this food took to get to your table?

You were designed to eat animal and plant matter that was alive right up to the moment you found it. This ensured that you would not only receive all the nutrients but also the life force imbued within the material. Numerous studies clearly show that the life force of plants is visible in vegetables and sprouts when photographed. This is vital energy that your body needs and is designed to consume. This is the energy of life, and it is easy to identify who is consuming it and who is not as the body ages. For this reason, it is best to select plant matter that is still in its original form, preferably with the dirt of field still visible upon it.

PRESERVATIVES ARE DOING EXACTLY THAT

You will note that nowhere in these discussions have we mentioned that the human body was designed to consume synthesized products. The creation and use of artificial preservatives, flavor enhancers, stabilizers, emulsifiers, and so on are a result of the industry that has sprung up around feeding an increasing population with no time or desire to prepare a meal. These products were created to increase the time a commodity remains edible after it has been harvested, to make it taste natural after it has been processed, or to make the product color or texture more appealing. None of them has anything to do with nourishing the body, and this should make you take notice. In fact, these products are approved for use in your food not because they provide additional nourishment but based on testing that shows they do not adversely affect your biology in the amounts tested. Repeated consumption of highly processed food acts as a weight within your physiology. As we have stated, consciousnesses ascending into fourth density will take their bodies with them. Continued ascension will become increasingly difficult if you are infusing your body with vibrationally suppressing chemicals ingested as you attempt to nourish it.

Knowing what to eat does not have to be a torturous path of wandering the aisles of the grocery store as you avoid the obstacles. Remember what was available when your body was designed and how that food was acquired and consumed. Listen to the feedback your body provides after you consume something. If you eat a meal and feel like it is dragging you down afterward, it should be obvious that your body is struggling to process it. If your food gives you indigestion or loose stools, that is an indication that your physiology is not compatible with something in that meal, and it is overcompensating as it tries to digest it.

You should feel energized after every meal as your body assimilates the nutrition and energy contained within it. The singular purpose for consuming matter is the acquisition of energy to sustain the vehicle until consciousness ascends and begins providing the required energy. The experience and perceived pleasure of taste is an instinctual program that must be identified as such and controlled as you continue your path of ascension.

NOURISHING THE MIND: YOU ARE WHAT YOU THINK YOU ARE

Our discussions thus far have shown that the power of consciousness has created the cosmos and everything that resides within it. The respective consciousnesses are responsible for the creations that exist within them. You are consciousness that is embodied as you read this text. You are therefore responsible for the body that resides within your toroidal sphere and the reality you are creating for yourself. You are here to learn lessons that provide balance and growth to your toroidal sphere, but the path you take as you navigate to those lessons—or miss them completely—is created through your intentions.

An infinite number of distractions will cause you to lose your focus if you allow them to do so. In addition to that, an endless stream of social programming attempts to mold your perceptions and condition you to respond a specific way to outside stimulus. These external influences begin to affect the narrative produced by the ego construct.

What Are Those Voices Inside Your Head Telling You?

Everyone has an internal compass that he or she steers by. The problem that sometimes occurs is that this compass is assumed to be accurate, when in fact it may have been thrown off by external influences. It is important to recognize this before it leads you so far off course that it becomes difficult to find your way back to the path toward your lessons. This usually manifests as an internal discussion that forms in your mind as if spoken from some hidden ventriloquist observing your thoughts and actions. Depending on the emotional state you find yourself in, this voice will praise, scorn, or create doubt. This is the ego construct in full control, attempting to direct your course when it is not qualified to do so. Many people have had this voice running wide open in their minds for so long that they no longer recognize it is there or how it is coloring their perceptions. The obvious first step is to realize that an internal narrative is occurring. Next you must become conscious of what it is telling you. Finally, you must begin to control and quiet the ramblings of the ego. This brings us to the final section of the book, where we will provide the tools that will assist and accelerate your ascension.

Part 4

MEDITATIONS AND MODALITIES

CHAPTER NINETEEN

The practice of meditation, or quiet mindfulness, has existed on Earth for thousands of years. It was brought here as a tool for ascension long before history was recorded. It is not limited to this construct; it's used throughout the cosmos as a way for embodied consciousness to seek higher understanding. We prefer the term quiet mindfulness to meditation because the concept of meditation has become a category in which all manner of discussions have been grouped. Like karma and sin, the definition has changed over time and is now molded into the shape that suits the purpose. For this reason, we will use quiet mindfulness as we describe the methods used to silence the ego programming and move into greater understanding.

Operating under a veil of forgetfulness with a programmed ego construct as you attempt to learn the lessons of balance is not a task to be completed in separation. For this reason, as consciousnesses begin to awaken, they are drawn to the concept that something beyond themselves exists. Quiet mindfulness is then seen as the pathway that will lead to inner knowledge of themselves and their existences.

The farther you look back into the recorded history of meditation, the more difficult and elaborate the methods appear to have been. Some requirements even went as far as to renounce the world and live a reclusive existence as disciples sought spiritual purity. While these sects still exist, the extreme measures they employ are no longer required to achieve the same results. The polarities on Earth have shifted toward the positive, and it is the negative that now is required to isolate and concentrate to preserve its polarity. Individual quiet mindfulness is no longer hindered by the thick frequency membrane of negativity that previously existed, and results are almost immediate.

The concept behind quiet mindfulness is to become aware of and silence the endless flow of ego-consciousness thought. Once you silence the programmed construct, you can then hear the rest of your consciousness—and the entirety of the universe. The first and most important aspect of quiet mindfulness is that you have consciously set the intention to seek a greater understanding of yourself and the cosmos in which you exist. It is a universal constant; answers arrive only after the questions have been asked.

Understanding Who You Really Are

Almost all of us understand there is more to our existence than the bodies we find ourselves in during our incarnations. What that "more" consists of is a point of debate because consciousness under the veil is deliberately kept from this knowledge. When your density and rotation reach a threshold of development, the energy it contains begins to bleed through the veil. This energy impacts your consciousness and drives you toward deeper understanding that is required for the next step of your journey. This is the marker of an ascending consciousness.

By the time your conscious energy is felt in this manner, you have already lived a multitude of lifetimes. These incarnations have given you the balance needed in your rotation. The actual number of lifetimes that you required to accomplish this is a function of the individual and the path you took to get there. From the perspective of individual consciousness in time-space, it makes no difference whether it required one hundred or one thousand lifetimes. From a galactic perspective, the longer it takes for this to occur on a planetary scale, the more it impacts the energy balance. A nonascending planet requires an equal offset in the opposing quadrant. It is therefore advantageous to rectify the issues holding consciousness back.

You have lived your life under the assumption that your personality is a product of your upbringing. However, once you achieve a threshold of conscious energy, another force comes into play. This has been defined as the steering current that leads you around lessons previously learned. Quieting the programmed ego construct of this lifetime allows you to access and understand the totality of your consciousness. As the ego recedes, the larger composite of your knowledge will assert itself. What you find within yourself as you peer into the depths is unique to the experience of your individual journey. As you continue to seek within, the understanding of who you really are comes into focus, and the fear of death falls away. This is a result of pushing your consciousness beyond the senses of the space-time body and into the time-space existence of consciousness. In time, you will be able to shift perspectives and look back upon your incarnation from this vantage point. This is a learned skill, and like any other, it will require practice and patience. How quickly you see results will depend on your desire and dedication. You will receive all that you invest.

Attaining quiet mindfulness does not require elaborate rituals or seclusion with gurus to teach you the proper way to do anything. You create your own reality; no one knows your creations better than you do. Focused intention results in manifestation. Beyond a few basic techniques to get you started and some knowledge of manipulating energy, you have free will to turn this into whatever you want. With that understanding, we will outline two meditation techniques to quiet the mind. We will then provide some intentions that will allow you to use and direct your energy appropriately. The exercises provided build upon each other to make them more effective. As you increase your density, you can then push the veil with more energy. As you push the veil, you will access higher knowledge, and so on. Once you begin to observe results from these activities, you will understand the feedback and can modify and create whatever you wish. This is graduation from third density.

CHAPTER TWENTY
THE FIRST MEDITATIONS OF QUIET MINDFULNESS

CANDLE FOCUS

This is the first exercise for those who have never attempted to quiet the mind; as such, it contains more discussion and steps. If you are already meditating, perhaps some of the perspectives offered will provide further insights. Take what is useful and allow that others may not be at your level and will benefit from the instruction.

Silencing the programmed construct requires effort relative to how dependent upon it you have been up to this point in your life. If it has been the dominant factor running unabated, it is going to be difficult to stop the incessant chatter. Like a child demanding attention, when you first ignore it, it will try anything to refocus your attention upon it. Like the spoiled child, once it understands the adult has asserted control, it will reluctantly accept its role. For this reason, an external focus is the first technique used to allow you to identify and ignore the internal dialogue as you concentrate upon it.

You will need a white candle with an exposed flame that you can comfortably observe from a sitting position. The wick should be trimmed so that the flame extends about an inch, creating a colorful, dancing light. Remove any buildup at the end of the wick, and if needed, remove some wax under the wick to achieve the proper wick height. Find a comfortable chair that you will not mind sitting in for the duration of this exercise. Your body should be in a state of satisfaction, where it is not demanding your attention. You should not be hungry, cold, uncomfortable, sick, or otherwise distracted by the needs of your body. You are attempting to disconnect your awareness from it, so you need to know it is okay while you ignore it.

Place the candle on a table in front of your chair, where you can observe the flame comfortably without straining the muscles in your neck. Light the candle and assume a comfortable position where you can remain motionless. Clear your mind of all thoughts. Your mind must remain quiet of conversation and empty of images during the entire exercise. Observe the outer edges of the flame and the motion that is created. Looking closer at the flame, you can see the variations of color that exist within it. Continue to observe the flame in this manner until your mind has been cleared of distraction for a discernible period—how long is up to you and your ability to quiet the mind and keep it quiet. It is during these first attempts at meditation that the untrained will suddenly find the inner voice of ego attempting to get their attention. You may find yourself thinking about a bill that needs to be paid or an event that recently occurred. You might be staring at the flame and suddenly realize you have been thinking about something. If this happens, it is the programmed construct attempting to regain control. If you do find yourself distracted by thoughts or conversation, continue to focus on the nuances of the flame as you silence the narrative and attain quiet mindfulness.

With your mind silenced, refocus your attention to the base of the flame, where it meets the wick. At the base of the flame there is a small spot of blackness; if it is not observable to you, imagine one where the flame meets the wick. This is the imagined creational energy interface between space-time and time-space. In your mind's eye, move your consciousness toward the black spot at the base of the flame. Observe that the black spot slowly expands as you move toward it. Your mind must remain empty during this process. If it is not empty, return to the perspective of a small black spot, and begin again. As your perspective moves to be encompassed by the blackness of the creational interface, close your eyes.

You now stand at the portal between the two realities. Set the intention that you desire access to the totality of your knowledge, and you will only accept the frequencies of unity and love. With this intention set, move your perspective through the portal and into the energy of the cosmos. You are now untethered consciousness, floating in the expanse of time-space. Distance does not exist here; manifestation is instantaneous. During these first experiences, keep your thoughts clear, and allow whatever happens to occur without judgment. Feel the serenity and peace of existence without concern as you float in the web of consciousness. What you experience here will be unique to you and exactly what you need at that moment.

When you are ready to end the journey, it is recommended to slowly exit rather than pop your eyes open and jolt yourself awake. No one likes the alarm clock shocking them out of a wonderful dream in the morning, and this is no different. As your journey in time-space ends, imagine that you are once again walking toward the portal between realities with the opposite perspective. Approach the portal, stop at the interface, and offer gratitude for whatever you experienced. As you emerge, become aware that you have stepped back into the sensations of your body. It is right where you left it and is waiting patiently for you. Feel your consciousness extend into your fingers and toes, reinvigorating and energizing them from the connection you have just shared with infinity. Open your eyes, and make note of how far the candle has burned. You should use this method until lighting and focusing upon the candle becomes a burden. The objective is to work up to thirty minutes of meditation and reduce the time required to walk through the portal.

GRADUATED QUIET MINDFULNESS

Once you become comfortable with quieting the mind, and you understand what a connection to your larger aspect feels like, you can discard the requirement of external focus to achieve it. As you continue to work with the connection, it will become easier to step through the portal, and whatever occurs once you are there will continue to evolve.

Allot the appropriate amount of time, and find a quiet location, free of distractions. All other considerations listed previously for the comfort of the body apply. Close your eyes, and envision the portal in front of you growing larger as you mentally approach it. Set the intention for a connection to unity and love, and allow the sensation to engulf you as you move through the portal into infinity. It is with this connection established that you will use the energy of creation through conscious intention, using the modalities that will be discussed next. End your session the same way as previously described, as you return your conscious focus to the body.

As you continue to work with this connection and the energy, you will be able to access it instantaneously when required. An example of this would be an interaction with negative polarity where you can feel the drain occurring. An immediate connection to creational energy will rebalance the equation in your favor.

USING THE ENERGY OF CREATION

In the discussions that follow, there will be numerous references to drawing the energy of creation into your consciousness. This is the energy of God Source and is used by all consciousnesses to manifest their creations within the universe. With the understanding that the observable universe exists within the toroidal sphere of God Source consciousness, the energy you are tapping exists as the charge between the photons that constitute God consciousness

(Figure 8). As you have seen thus far, this energy is not a mystical force that exists in an unidentified ether, where the faithful receive its bounty through hardship and self-sacrifice. It is a scientifically explainable energy available to anyone not completely drenched in negative polarity. From this position of understanding, you can observe the mechanics behind the concepts of quiet mindfulness and exactly what energy you draw into your consciousness. Pulling creational energy into the center of your consciousness is what occurs on a galactic level as the first planetary systems are created within it. If creational energy has this ability, it will certainly perform the tasks we are about to discuss.

CHAPTER TWENTY-ONE

HARNESSING CREATIONAL ENERGY

CLEARING THE SPHERE OF CONSCIOUSNESS

The connection to your higher aspect during quiet mindfulness allows you to interface with creational energy. This energy can then be directed and used through deliberate intention. Again, the cosmos gives you what you ask for, but you must first know what you need. Consciousness exists within a rotating toroidal sphere, and the interaction between photons creates a barrier membrane around the periphery. We have discussed the interactions and transfer of energy that occur between polarized consciousnesses. This exchange occurs automatically until you understand that you have the energy and ability to prevent it. The techniques presented below will realign any negativity that exists within your consciousness and dissipate any creations that you may have unknowingly created. Advanced techniques are beyond the scope of this book and will be presented in a subsequent publication.

NEGATIVE POLARITY

We have described negative polarity as a reverse rotational energy that enters your toroidal sphere in the same manner as an infection enters the body. Once inside your consciousness, negativity creates reverse-rotating, oppositely charged photons that then unbalance your rotation. If the infection continues, your rotation will become increasingly unbalanced, and you will begin physically manifesting what is occurring in your consciousness. Negative polarity can be removed from your consciousness through intentional realignment using the positive energy of creation.

TRAVELERS

During your lifetime you may have collected a few unwanted *travelers* that you have no idea you are nourishing with your energy. Negatively aligned consciousness exists both individually and collectively. They can reduce the positivity within you when they are in your proximity if they contain the larger potential. This is an external force acting upon your consciousness, and they cannot enter the barrier membrane. The unwanted travelers we are describing are the ones you have unknowingly created yourself that now exist within the sphere of your consciousness.

We previously described how a galactic consciousness creates systems of planetary life within the sphere of its consciousness and you have the same ability on a much smaller scale. The fact that you are doing this unconsciously and allowing the resulting travelers to reside within your sphere is irrelevant. The important thing is to become aware of whatever you may have created, dissolve it, rebalance your toroidal rotation, and regain the energy.

The creation of travelers occurs because of your continued focus upon a person or an event. As you continually focus your thoughts upon this thing, you give it energy. With continued focus, you will eventually create a barrier membrane around a section of your photonic array. You then have given a separate subidentity to whatever this thing is that you are fixating upon. The more you focus upon the thing, the more energy you give to your creation. If you are always looking backward and lamenting bad experiences, or you hold resentments against people who have committed perceived transgressions, you may have multiple travelers. Now consider the energy these creations require to remain intact and continue their existence.

If you do nothing with these creations during your lifetime, they will be dissolved in the etheric of the collective as the veil of forgetfulness is removed. They exist within the veil and cannot withstand the energy required to remove the partition. If they can be dissolved in the etheric, they can be dissolved now through conscious intention and a connection to creational energy.

EXERCISE

Establish your connection to quiet mindfulness through one of the methods previously listed. When you arrive beyond the portal, rather than floating around and waiting to see what happens, focus your attention on a perspective at the center of your toroidal sphere. You are looking out from the center and can see all that is you. Columns extend above and below your awareness as they reach out and connect to the outer rotating sphere (Figure 6).

From this perspective, you can see and interact with the entirety of your consciousness. Imagine the rotation that occurs as the energy of your experience causes the photons to oscillate. The flow should be smooth and unrestricted; you can feel the effortless movement as the photons move up the column and down along the outside of the sphere. With the rotation of your consciousness envisioned, draw creational energy downward into the column through the top of your perspective. The energy is a golden light that collects at the center of your consciousness.

As you continue to pull energy into your center, it shines outward, soaking your consciousness. You can feel the frequency of creational love energy coursing through the entirety of your consciousness as you realign any polarity not in unity and release any creations you may have created. Set the intention: You have been realigned and cleared of anything that might have existed through the deliberate action of creational energy. You know it, you feel it, and there is no doubt. Remain in this energy, if you like. There is no limit other than the one you impose. You end the session using the same method previously described to slowly awaken.

From this moment forward, do not fixate upon past events or perceived wrongs committed against you by others. It is far better to accept the experience—whatever it may be—and move forward, enriched by the lesson it provided without assigning a polarity to it. Undue focus upon something creates these travelers that are then cleared through this process. You now have a method to dissipate them, but it is better to move beyond the need for their creation through an understanding of consciousness.

ESTABLISHING A BARRIER

All consciousnesses create a barrier membrane around their rotating spheres. This membrane is created through the energetic oscillations that occur because of the photonic spin, frequency, and vibrational rate. This membrane encapsulates the unique experience of the consciousness by surrounding the entire array. Without an understanding of the operation of this membrane, it remains porous and allows polarity exchanges to occur unabated, as higher-order energies realign lower. From an unaware embodied consciousness standpoint, this is experienced as emotional and mood changes that seem to happen without reason. As you work in consciousness, you will become sensitive to the energies that others carry and will be able to hold your space against unwanted exchanges.

In a previous discussion, we gave an example of an experience in a waiting room, where a negative consciousness changed the outlook of a positive consciousness. If the positive consciousness had established a barrier prior to the interaction, the results may have been different. Establishing a barrier sets the intention through energy that you are not going to participate in random exchanges any longer. Overpowering magnitudes of polarity will require shielding, which will be discussed next.

EXERCISE

Using the same method for clearing your toroidal sphere, enter quiet mindfulness, and set your perspective at the center of your consciousness. Again, begin by drawing creational energy into the center of your consciousness. Begin to visualize yourself stretching your awareness to the very edges of all that is you. You can see the magnetic barrier membrane that surrounds you as a golden shield. Looking closer, you can see that this golden shield is energy that moves with undulating spikes that peak and ebb as they extend outward from your shield, like spears. As you observe the movement, you see that some spikes extend farther than others, and there are spots without any spikes at all. This is the barrier membrane your consciousness has produced without any effort on your part. The flat spots represent unbalanced openings, where polarity exchanges occur that you will now correct.

With the energy of creation that you previously acquired, you will now set the intention to smooth and balance your barrier. You can feel the energy radiating outward through your consciousness like a warm embrace. Any imbalances within your photonic array are removed as this energy moves toward your golden barrier membrane. As the energy permeates the membrane, you can see the spikes are all becoming the same size. The larger spikes shrink as new spikes appear, where previously there were none. Continue to observe the smoothing until all the spikes are the same size and no gaps remain. Feel the peace and satisfaction within you as you exist in unity with God Source creational energy. Set the intention that this is the only energy you will allow to penetrate your barrier. As you observe your newly sculpted barrier, you understand that you will feel energy more efficiently, now that it has been properly aligned. You will feel energy, and nothing will be allowed to penetrate without your permission. You know it, you feel it, and there is no doubt. Exist here as long as you like. When you are finished, end the session through the slow-awakening process.

This is a cleansing technique. You should perform it regularly for maintenance and if you feel you have been impacted by an undesired energy that might require realignment.

SHIELDING

This section is required due to the polarities that still exist on Earth. We have provided the mechanics of polarity interaction and how an overpowering polarity will realign the lower when in proximity. As you work with the concepts provided in this book, you will become sensitive to polarity imbalances and will feel them as they begin to pull at your consciousness. If the negative polarity is of a large enough magnitude, it will absorb positivity, even through a balanced barrier membrane. In this instance, you must identify what is occurring and stop it, or withdraw from the energy—or both, depending on the magnitude encountered. Unless you are adept in energy work, we recommend that when the feeling of being drained occurs, you use the shielding technique below and remove yourself from the source at your earliest opportunity.

When you reactivate the ability to sense the energy others are carrying, negative polarity will become obvious. The easiest way to begin opening your awareness is to watch for people who are outwardly angry or in a bad mood. As they come within your proximity, open your awareness to how they make you feel as they walk by. Even with no verbal or physical interaction, you should be able to feel the negativity impacting your barrier membrane. If you do not feel anything right away, that's okay. This aspect of your senses has been shut down through the separation that exists between the programmed ego construct and your consciousness beyond the veil. It will take some practice and exercise to get it working again. When you do feel it, you will be able to identify it from that moment forward. Everyone is unique, but some physical descriptions of the sensations that might be felt are a cold draft entering your consciousness, a darkness that attempts to envelop your light, a reflexive repulsion to something intangible, anger seeping into you for no reason, or a sudden feeling of fatigue, as if your energy is being drawn away. If you already have aligned your barrier membrane and still feel these sensations, you are in the proximity of an overpowering polarity.

The previous exercise balanced and aligned your barrier membrane to protect you from random environmental factors associated with the interactions between consciousnesses. If you are still impacted, additional measures will be required. To stop the transfer, you must use the manifested intention of your conscious energy to disallow the process. You will create a temporary impermeable shield out of your barrier membrane through your intention. The most effective way to do this is with your eyes closed, focusing on your conscious sphere, as you would during quiet mindfulness. If you find yourself in a situation where you cannot safely keep your eyes closed, perform the following process repeatedly as often as you can safely shut your eyes.

EXERCISE

Close your eyes and envision the totality of your consciousness, with you at the center within the seat of consciousness, the rotating sphere beyond it, and the golden barrier membrane surrounding all of it. Take a deep breath, and feel the warmth of creational energy being drawn into your center as you do this. As you exhale, envision yourself forcefully pushing white creational energy into your barrier membrane. As this occurs the membrane solidifies into a golden shield that will not allow any energy transfers between your consciousness and any other. Repeat this exercise as many times as you feel is required. As you open your eyes, you must remain focused on the solidified barrier you have created until you no longer are in proximity of the polarity drain. Continued use of this method for long periods requires conscious energy, and it will fatigue you. How quickly you tire will be a factor of the density and energy of consciousness that you carry.

As the polarities continue to shift toward the positive on Earth, a clear line will form. Generally, positive consciousness that is unaware it is harboring negativity is cleared of the infection by consciousnesses deliberately sharing creational energy. As this process accelerates the unknowingly polarized will be cleared, and the remaining consciousnesses continuing to harbor negativity will be of increasing magnitude. It is ill advised to attempt to shield for long periods of time when you are in proximity of overpowering entities. A better course of action would be to shield, identify the source of the drain, and remove yourself from proximity.

DELIBERATELY SHARING CREATIONAL ENERGY (LOVE)

You have learned how to pull creational energy into your consciousness to realign it and how to create a barrier to exclude negative polarity intrusions. We have thus far concentrated upon the individual to properly align you to the creational energy of God Source. As consciousness ascends and aligns to the energies of creation, separation naturally falls away. You cannot exist in the energy that is responsible for all creation and not feel the connection to everything that has been created. As you begin to understand the interconnected nature of existence and the construct we all reside within, the reality becomes undeniable. At the origin of consciousness is the photon that has been donated by and exists within God Source consciousness. The individuality of consciousness is a gift; ascending in consciousness is a gift; knowledge is a gift; existing in the unity of God Source creational energy is a gift; and gifts are meant to be given and shared. Ultimately, you share your gifts with yourself as you assist the perceived separate consciousnesses with which you are embodied. At the end of embodiment, you all will ascend into the same collective consciousness.

On Earth, separations can be found in almost any corner of existence. These separations have been cultivated because under the veil of forgetfulness, the fertilizer of self-interest allowed these weeds to take root. You separate yourselves under flags, skin color, language, religions, social class, and every other difference you can identify. Have you ever stopped to consider how and why these constructs were created? From an ascended perspective, these perceived separations are ridiculous. You are all consciousness, embodied in a human vehicle on Earth, and you are all the same. The differences you observe and the separations you embrace are a result of the influence of polarity. As we have stated, the primary objective of negative polarity is to create division that impedes unity, which must then be overcome by a determined positive collective. It is time to release the division and realign it by sharing creational energy with all you encounter.

Consider the concept of road rage that occurs when one consciousness creates a perceived transgression against another motorist. Do you get angry as a response because this person has just impeded your progress by a few seconds? If you do, is it justified or a conditioned emotional response that you instinctually fell into? Or did you perhaps find it humorous that the individual would act illogically for no apparent reason? The answer, of course, depends upon your polarity, which affects your mood, and the response you choose to embrace. Consider another interaction, this one on a personal level. You are in a grocery store, pushing your basket along as you acquire the components for your meals. As you are distracted by the cookies on the shelf, you bump into the cart of another shopper. The other shopper has had a very bad week and responds in anger to your mistake. How do you respond? In both cases the proper response is to remain in a positive creational energy space and consciously share the energy of love with the other person to realign and clear his or her negativity. This is a simple process; with an understanding of the mechanics involved comes the knowledge of how important and beneficial it is to those you clear.

Sharing your energy to realign negativity can be automatic through proximity. Just walking through a crowd as you consciously exude love and light will leave a path of realignment in your wake. Responding to an overtly angry individual can be done through a focused intention or a touch to realign the hostility. This is the same concept as the resonant action that occurs between two power lines in proximity. While they are not touching, the electromagnetic fields still interact. Touching these two lines together, however, produces an interaction of far greater magnitude.

Shaking hands is an accepted practice during reconciliation and will provide the most opportunity for realigning negativity. During the encounter, it is important to remain in a space of peace and love and not allow yourself to be triggered. While you are in proximity, you consciously radiate creational energy as you set the intention to realign the negative. Outwardly, you do and say whatever is necessary to deescalate the situation. Unless physical harm is imminent, de-escalation should always be the objective. There is no side to stand on, no pride to defend, no sensibilities to be offended, no division of any kind to be embraced. There is only the unity of God Source energy and the polarity attempting to negate it. If you do maneuver the situation to a conciliatory handshake, as you shake hands, feel the energy leaving your hand and moving into your new friend as you share the gift of realignment.

Rumors abound of Chinese adepts who cultivate and focus their internal energy, termed qi or chi. Videos even exist that show what appear to be unbelievable feats of consciousness being performed as they manipulate the construct and the actions of others. As previously mentioned, the Chinese have mapped the energy conduits of the human vehicle and these techniques exist with a body of knowledge that has been closely guarded until recently. This is the same energy that we are discussing and providing methods to harness. It is not a secret; it is the operation of ascending consciousnesses gaining control of their reality, and we have scientifically explained it to you. It is available to all who properly apply themselves, have the rotational balance, and can exist within the creational energy of God Source.

This energy is of a positive nature and cannot be warped to fulfill self-serving interests or cause harm beyond defending free-will incursions. The adepts who study these arts discovered long ago that the energy available decreases the farther consciousness strays from purity. This energy is available to all who seek it and is what we describe when we talk of energy exchanges realigning negativity during touch.

At no point have we said that you should allow negative polarity to force its will upon you. In fact, the galactic solution to the negative polarity infection was to eradicate it, using its own creations. There is a difference between defusing and deescalating a situation and allowing actions against your will. Create your realities accordingly.

MANUALLY EXPANDING YOUR PHOTONIC DENSITY

The awareness that you identify as your consciousness is composed of photons. These photons store the energy of experience as electromagnetic energy that causes them to spin and vibrate. When a photon becomes saturated with as much energy as it can hold, the frequency of spin and vibration become so intense that a single photon will divide into two photons. Each photon will contain half of the energy that the single photon contained before division (Figure 4). As consciousness ascends and gains an understanding of the construction of consciousness and the cosmos they inhabit, a new ability becomes available—manual expansion of conscious density. This ability begins slowly so that you may work with it as you ascend beyond third-density embodiment.

Prior to achieving the required aggregate density, photonic division occurs automatically through the energy of experience and not much else. This is because your consciousness does not contain the proper rotational stability and architecture to adequately charge and release the creational energy required for photonic division. Consciousness that engages with this book initially will have a limited ability to manually expand its density through focused intention. Repeated practice with the exercises will increase its effectiveness, and over a period of use, you will notice changes in your abilities. How those changes manifest depends on the path of the individual. Remain vigilant, and the internal changes will become evident.

As you ascend into upper fourth density, the need to consume matter for energy will fall away. Absorbing creational energy then becomes the primary conduit for reenergizing the body and consciousness. Fourth density is a transitional phase that allows you to familiarize and acclimate to the new nourishment source. When you ascend beyond the need for embodiment, absorbing creational energy will be your source of nourishment. Your first creations in the etheric will mimic your memories of embodiment, and you will therefore create the illusion that you are consuming this energy as a liquid in one manner or another. The need for that will also fall away as your ascension continues.

The laws of matter that you observe in your material construct do not apply beyond fourth density. The principles of thermodynamics and physics exist within the material planes and are a function of coalesced creational energy (material constructs) interacting with consciousness. The interaction creates graviton waves, resulting from the resistance to movement inside the toroidal sphere. This creates the space-time lock, which in turn creates the limitations you observe. Consciousness is the ultimate construct in which all else exists. Ascension requires that you begin to enrich yourselves through the utilization of creational energy. This will increase your density, and when you ascend as a collective beyond the threshold, you will cease being a consumer of this energy and will become a producer. The energy you produce will then be lovingly supplied to the energy web, where it will nourish those who require it for their growth. This is the energy balance of the cosmos that we have discussed in this book, and it's the reason this information has been provided.

To expand your density, you must have practiced enough with quiet mindfulness that you can achieve a clear connection without effort. As you become practiced in the technique, you will find your way to the connection almost immediately, anywhere, regardless of the exterior distractions that may exist. It is with repetition that a lesson becomes a skill.

EXERCISE

For this exercise we recommend that you stand with your feet shoulder-width apart, with your arms outstretched and palms facing outward. You will use the energy pathways of your body as a lightning rod to attract, store, and redirect creational energy through your consciousness. Standing in the sunlight is useful as you first begin working with this technique. Creational energy is directed through the sun to provide the nourishment required for the physical creations. You are interested in the photonic energy that will bombard you, physically sensed in the form of light and heat. The physical sensations provide a focus to concentrate upon and will accelerate the positive feedback. As you become familiar with the technique, you will find that it works regardless of the solar input, but the results vary between individuals, and free photonic energy is always a pleasant gift.

Using the method previously discussed, enter a state of quiet mindfulness and align your perspective to the seat of consciousness at the center of your toroidal sphere. In this instance, the center of your toroidal sphere remains with your embodied conscious awareness, right behind your eyes. As you stand in the sun, begin to feel it upon your body, energizing it as the energy penetrates and warms your skin. You are setting the intention to open your energy system to creational God Source energy.

Envision the main energy network that exists within your body as a large conduit that runs from your head down into your groin. This main conduit has discreet energy nodes (chakras) within it that connect to smaller conduits that extend throughout every part of your body. As the energy from the sun warms your skin, you can feel the energy moving through the smaller channels of your body toward the main conduit. You can feel this energy building, swelling the chakra energy nodes as it collects there. You intend to collect as much energy as you can hold. Stay in this intention until you think you are full.

With your hands outstretched, palms outward, take a deep breath as you move your arms inward. Your hands should meet, finger to finger, without touching, just below your belly button. As a single motion, continue to move your hands upward toward your heart as you visualize the energy you have collected being pushed up the main conduit toward your heart chakra. Exhale as you turn your hands, and push the energy out of your heart chakra to the edges of your barrier membrane as if you were pushing something away from you to your left and right. While you move your hands, see the energy as a golden bubble that you push outward through your consciousness. As this energy moves through your photonic array, you can feel it energizing and increasing the spin of each photon. After a few energy pushes, you can feel the photons that were at saturation starting to divide. Your energy is growing and expanding; you feel it, you know it, and there is no doubt. Repeat this process as many times as you like. To end the session, raise your arms in a Y above your body. Take a deep breath and pull your hands down until they are finger to finger over your heart. Exhale as you push downward along the main energy conduit, and let your hands sweep out past your body. As you do this, you are in a space of gratitude as you set the intention to close your energy system and protect it once again from unwanted energies.

Pushing the Veil

The veil of forgetfulness is a tool employed to assist lower third-density consciousness as it repeatedly incarnates to gain the lessons of balance. The veil can be likened to an instinctual second-density behavior that is understood and controlled when it is no longer useful. To push the veil of forgetfulness, you must first understand that it is a partition erected within your consciousness and not something external and intangible. Once you become aware that this partition within you is keeping your programmed ego consciousness separated from the rest of your experiences, you have crossed the first hurdle required to remove it. Pushing the veil is a slow and deliberate process that requires effort. You are not going to perform this exercise a few times and have access to the entirety of your experiences. You still have lessons to learn, or you would not be here. Access to everything without regard to how it would impact your path would be a disservice.

As you set the intention to push the veil, what you can access will be a function of what the totality of your consciousness thinks is appropriate. This will not result in a clear recollection of prior lifetimes but as a gradual shift in your conscious perspective. As you continue to work with this exercise, your dreams may become more vivid as the deeply ingrained experiences begin to resurface. The subconscious is a much softer platform to relay experiences through, and it is here that you will need to pay attention. If the experience is too much for the operative consciousness, a dream is easily disregarded as fiction. This gives you a medium where you can sort what is helpful and discard what is not. For this reason, it is suggested that you keep paper and pen or pencil near your bed to record your dreams; write what you remember immediately upon waking.

Exercise

This is another exercise where you must have practiced enough with quiet mindfulness that you can achieve a clear connection without effort. Find a quiet spot for your seated exercise, and prepare as you normally would. Close your eyes and envision the totality of your consciousness, with you at the center within the seat of consciousness, the rotating sphere beyond it, and the golden barrier membrane surrounding all of it. As you observe the totality of your consciousness, you will become aware of another golden barrier that is just outside your viewing perspective at the seat of consciousness. Now that you can see this barrier, you will feel it also, as if it were a hat that previously fit, but you've outgrown it, and it's now too tight. With the barrier clearly visible, pull creational energy into your center as you take a deep breath. As you forcibly exhale, imagine that the seat of your consciousness is a balloon that is expanding and pushing on the barrier uniformly in all directions. Repeat this process, and as the balloon of consciousness continues to expand, it pushes the barrier outward. It is advisable to perform this exercise directly after you complete the expanding-your-density exercise. Your consciousness will be brimming with energy and primed for optimal results. End this exercise in the same slow and deliberate manner as the other exercises.

Continue this process as long as you feel comfortable, but be advised that it will eventually tire you. You are using conscious energy to forcibly push an electromagnetic barrier. How quickly you tire will be a function of the amount of conscious energy that you can store within your toroidal array. Repeated practice with increasing your density and then pushing the barrier will yield greater results as you progress along the ascending path and become fluent in the processes.

Chapter Twenty-Two

RECONNECTING TO YOUR SELF-HEALING ABILITY

The timeline that you exist within is immersed in separation. The manifestation of self-interest associated with negativity has pushed this agenda and caused separation in almost every aspect of embodiment. As a result, consciousness operating under the veil has forgotten the connection to the self-healing abilities that it naturally possesses. This can be restored as you remember what you are and how to operate your consciousness.

There are stories of humans in your recorded history who lived upon Earth in a single body for hundreds of years. If you take a quick look at the current expected lifespan, an odd disparity comes into focus. If these stories are to be believed, what mechanisms changed that dramatically shortened the lifespan of the human vehicle? If they are fabrications, why would anyone create such an obvious deception and continue to include it in manuscripts that have been revised and reprinted thousands of times? If one part of a story is an obvious fabrication, it creates suspicion that the rest of the information also might be false. The reality is that these stories have been handed down through the generations orally and through recovered writings. Some omissions and translational errors have occurred as facts are embellished to add interest and boring details discarded. A thread of truth does remain within the tales, however, and we now will weave that into the abilities that you can recover.

Universally, consciousness is a toroidal sphere of photons that use creational energy to coalesce matter within their influence. You are no different, and the body you currently inhabit exists within your sphere of consciousness. There are limitations to embodiment in the Earth construct, and you agreed to them before your incarnation. There are constructs within galaxies, where a body is engineered in a factory, and your consciousness attached to it so you can interact within the material planes. The limitations of existence placed upon that body depend upon the length of your mission. On Earth, your body is created and grown within the conscious sphere of another. As you attach your consciousness to the growing body, it then becomes a cooperative effort until you are separated and take ownership. It is not a coincidence that some mothers are said to be glowing and radiant as they approach the birth of their children. The energy of two consciousnesses are existing together, and the observable results depend upon the energy and balance each contain.

The current observations of aging on Earth are of a body that grows into maturity, exists for a brief period in youthful vitality, and slowly loses that vitality at an accelerating rate until death. From an embodied consciousness perspective, you fully develop your ego programming during the youthful vitality phase. Your consciousness then becomes confused as it watches the body age while it still feels as if it should be in a youthfully vibrant body. The rapid aging that has occurred is a result of several factors; the most notable was the negative polarity membrane that has existed for thousands of years hindering the access of consciousness to revitalizing creational energy. This membrane is collapsing, and consciousness is recovering the ability to connect to it and utilize the energy that is its photonic birthright. The other factor is that as a collective, you have forgotten how to operate in consciousness. As you fell deeper into the abyss of separation and self-interest, you identified solely as the ego construct and lost contact with the totality of your consciousness that exists beyond the veil. This section will help you reconnect to the ability of consciousness to maintain the vitality of the vehicle that it inhabits.

Your body exists within the toroidal sphere of your consciousness that is anchored at your heart center. Consciousness is responsible for the material creations that exist within it, and this includes your body. While you may not be aware of it, the health and vitality of your body depends on many factors, seen and unseen. The environmental factors associated with nourishment, toxic chemical burdens, and use of the body are the material considerations of the construct. The unseen factor is the energy you receive from your consciousness that maintains the vehicle. This energy is supplied through the main energy conduit that runs from your head to your groin, with smaller lines connected to energy nodes that reach to every part of your body. When this channel is activated and used with conscious intent, the body receives the creational energy it needs and is in contact with the energetic blueprint from which it was created.

THE BLUEPRINT OF YOUR PERFECTED SELF

Over the course of your repeating lifetimes, you have created an energetic blueprint for the human form that exists within your consciousness. This blueprint is more appropriately called an energy template that you will follow as you shape the body you will inhabit. As you select the point of your incarnation, the energy template is modified slightly, according to the genetic profile of the source material supplied and which gender you have chosen. There are some limitations of the genetic material that cannot be overwritten, but overall, you are in control of your reality. Keep in mind that you chose—or understood and accepted—whatever limitations you observed as you grew into maturity. This discussion does not include outside factors that have caused mutations to the genetic material, accidents that deform the body, or other outside factors that limit or otherwise handicap the body. Some of these may have been intentional lesson paths, but the concept of accidents previously discussed applies here. While you may be unaware of it, the energy template of your perfect form exists within your consciousness and is waiting for you to connect to it and use creational energy to heal yourself.

The template of your perfect form is a translucent grid of energy pathways, organs, bone, and muscle. This appears as varying intensities of a golden hue, which represents the energy of creation in perfect alignment with the original design of your body. The main energy conduit is a blinding golden-white light that signifies the entry of the creational energy into your template that energizes the network. As it moves into the smaller conduits, they are observed as pulsing with golden light as the energy is transmitted to the rest of the body. The organs, bone, and muscle appear as fuzzy golden outlines as they are energized. This is the template that your body was intended to become when you reached maturity. It is also the template that provides the ability to maintain the body far beyond any current expectations of youth. There are still some limitations to what can be achieved, due to the polarities that still exist on Earth, but this impediment is subsiding. When the constructs diverge, and consciousness ascends into fourth-density embodiment on Earth, the exercise below will produce increasing results. Your body will then maintain its youthful vigor longer, and life spans will steadily increase as you exist in unmolested unity with creational energy.

EXERCISE

For this exercise, stand facing the sun with your feet shoulder-width apart and your arms outstretched, palms facing outward. The physical sensations of heat provide a focus to concentrate on and will accelerate the positive feedback. As you become familiar with these techniques, you will find that it works regardless of the solar input, but the results vary between individuals.

Using the method previously discussed, enter a state of quiet mindfulness and align your perspective to the seat of consciousness at the center of your toroidal sphere. From this vantage point, you can see the sphere of your consciousness completely enveloping your entire body, as your body exists within the column that runs from top to bottom. As you stand in the sun, feel it upon your body, knowing that it is energizing your entire consciousness as the energy penetrates it and warms your skin. Inhale and bring your hands together, finger to finger in front of your belly button. Raise them together in a cupping fashion until they are over your heart. Exhale as you extend them straight out until your arms are completely extended at shoulder height, with palms outward. You are setting the intention to open your energy system to your total consciousness and realign with your template of perfection. Maintain this posture, arms outstretched as you feel yourself bathing in the energies.

Envision the main energy network within your body—the large conduit connected within the column of consciousness, and the rest of the network as it distributes the energy to your body. From your perspective at the seat of consciousness, your perfected energy template materializes just in front of you. You can see the golden energy of your perfected form, shimmering as it comes closer and slowly envelops your body. As you stand in the sun, you can feel the energy coursing through the template as it energizes and integrates with your body, realigning anything that does not match it. The template is now completely meshed with your internal energy network, and you can see the golden filaments radiating healing energy throughout your body. You can feel it coursing through you as the warmth fills every atom of your being. You may feel twitching or minor body movements as the creational energy realigns any imperfections, opens blockages, and meshes with the coalesced creational energy that is the structure of your organic body.

Using a part of your consciousness, follow the energy as it flows from the creational energy web into your crown chakra, down your spine, through your arms, and out of the tips of your fingers, into your heart and vital organs, down your legs, and finally into the earth through the soles of your feet. As this occurs, set the intention that this energy is revitalizing, repairing, and realigning you to your perfected self. You know it, you feel it, and there is no doubt. Repeat this step as many times as you wish, but this is another exercise that requires directed conscious energy and will eventually tire you.

To end the session, raise your arms in a Y above your body. Take a deep breath, and pull your hands down until they are finger to finger over your heart. Exhale as you push downward along the main energy conduit, and let your hands sweep out past your body. As you do this, you are in a space of gratitude as you set the intention to close your energy system and protect it once again from unwanted energies.

You should stand as you perform this exercise until you are comfortable with the process. You may then lie horizontally on your back, with your limbs uncrossed, as you perform the visualizations. This will allow you to stay in the energies longer without physically fatiguing the body. Your energy systems should not be bent or otherwise restricted for this work to provide optimal results.

CONNECTING TO YOUR HIGHER ASPECT

The discussions in this book have alluded to the fact that higher self or higher aspect can be a misleading concept. The following is a definition summary:

- If you are third-density organic consciousness, you evolved in this construct and are not a fragmented consciousness and therefore do not have a larger portion of yourself existing at a higher station. What you do have is consciousness within your rotation that exists beyond the veil you currently are under, and it can provide guidance.
- Organic third-density consciousness that has achieved the required density but not the required balance for ascension will have access to a guide, or group of guides who are fourth-density entities, helping it tidy up and ascend.
- Fragmented consciousness is a portion of an ascended consciousness that has decided to re-experience embodiment. In this case, the consciousness will have access to whatever level of ascension its totality of consciousness has attained.

One is not better than the other, beyond the clarity of information that can be accessed and the perspective from which information is viewed. The other point previously discussed is that you will not gain access to information that might impede the path toward the lessons you came here to learn. This does not mean that you never will have access; instead, it means that the knowledge you acquire will be metered. As you progress through your lessons, more knowledge may then become available. In fact, one of your lessons may be the acquisition of higher-order knowledge so that it can be shared.

The construct of Earth requires that everyone follows the same rules, and all incarnated consciousnesses have agreed to this. The rules are forgetfulness, duality, polarity, and separation. To access higher levels of understanding, ascended consciousnesses must first successfully navigate the distractions as they are immersed in the construct. If they successfully awaken to their intended paths, they will ask for deeper knowledge. When they have a connection to a source that can provide that knowledge, it will flow. Perhaps you are reading this book to awaken to a purpose beyond what the programmed ego can currently comprehend. Many will.

EXERCISE

In a quiet location, where you will not be bothered, enter a state of quiet mindfulness from a sitting position. Observe yourself as a rotating sphere of consciousness, floating in the nothingness of time-space. You can clearly see the golden shimmering of your barrier membrane as it interacts with the creational energy web. The creational energy web exists in unity with God Source, and you can feel the loving embrace as unity washes through you. Negativity cannot exist here, and you will not accept anything that is not in unity with this energy. You are in a state of blissful existence, and it feels as if you could exist here forever.

As wonderful as this is, there is somewhere that you need to go. You are not sure where you are going or who is there, but you know that others have been waiting for you to call on them. Begin repeating the following silent intention: "I am going home." Continue to say this in your consciousness; it is the only thing in your mind—you are going home. As you concentrate on going home, you now realize that you are moving through the energy web. As you continue to repeat the intention, you accelerate; you are going somewhere.

The movement slows as another consciousness sphere comes into view. Feel the energy signature of this consciousness; it should feel as if you have just found a missing piece of yourself. Expand your awareness beyond your barrier membrane as you extend your energy like a handshake. As you do this, visualize a whirlpool of energy that extends from the barrier of your consciousness and connects to the barrier of the other consciousnesses. Only love and unity energy can flow through this connection, and you will not accept anything else. Set the silent intention that you are ready to establish a connection with the other portion of your consciousness that you have just found, and then sit in a silent space of receptivity for a few minutes. Repeat this process until something happens. The response you receive will depend on the path you are on and will be exactly what you need. You may get a response in the first attempt, or you may have to repeat this exercise and the others provided in this book several times before a response is given. Eventually, you will connect.

To end the exercise, retract your consciousness back inside your barrier membrane. Give thanks for whatever information you were given. If you did not connect, sit in a space of gratitude for having the knowledge to attempt this as you slowly return from your journey and reorient yourself back into your body. Awaken using the slow and deliberate method previously described.

Chapter Twenty-three

ACCESSING HIGHER-ORDER ABILITIES

As embodied consciousness, several considerations must be addressed when discussing abilities beyond what is currently associated with the five senses. Your body has been designed to ascend with your consciousness, and additional abilities become available as the energy of consciousness pushes their activation. The energy network of your body is designed to collect and utilize creational energy that has been acquired through deliberate focus. The ability to focus this energy requires the density and rotational balance to collect and push creational energy from the etheric plane into the systems of matter that are your body and the space-time it exists within. Knowledge of how to access and pull this creational energy must be sought by the individual as their consciousnesses push them toward awakening. This is the process of ascension; additional capabilities become available as you reach the conscious maturity to seek them and use them correctly. The information and exercises contained in this book will assist you in this goal. As you expand and balance your consciousness using the information provided, you will reach a level where the activation of your energy systems provides physical feedback. What that feedback consists of will be as unique as you are within the vastness of the cosmos.

The other aspect of abilities within the physical is the proper alignment of the body you have created. The organism that is the body must be properly nourished and maintained to operate at a level where higher-order abilities can manifest. The body is exposed to numerous products in your current environment that cause a reduction of vibrational capacitance. This, simply stated, means that your body is then unable to properly connect and utilize the energy of your consciousness. If your body loses the connection to the template of your perfect body, it will continue to repair itself according to the biological coding of the genetic materials. If you ingest and absorb toxic chemicals, over time they damage these codes, and disorders manifest. Without the proper information to correct the damage, the body attempts to repair itself using genetic information that has changed, and it strays farther from the perfected state. Access to higher-order abilities will depend on your alignment to them in body and consciousness. Both operate in unison to create a collector and an antenna that allow higher-order functions to be made manifest. As this occurs within an increasing number of individuals, they become the light along the path that others will follow.

This book has provided specific guidance related to the considerations of the body and exercises for the expansion of consciousness. When used together, they will lead you to higher-order abilities. What you receive from these exercises will be in direct proportion to the amount of conscious energy you invest and your belief in yourself. The historical programming of this construct is filled with information that suggests this is impossible. You must ascend beyond these limitations and understand the magnificence of what you are and the unlimited abilities that are waiting for you to claim them.

HYPNOTHERAPY AND PAST-LIFE REGRESSION AS A TOOL OF ACCELERATION

We have defined the veil of forgetfulness as a magnetic partition that has been erected within your consciousness. This partition allows you to create an ego program that has no knowledge of the larger experiences that are contained within your consciousness beyond the veil. As you begin third-density awareness, you operate within this partition and identify as the ego program and nothing more. As your lifetimes accrue, the energy of your consciousness begins to exert an outside pressure upon the veil, and guidance begins to bleed through. Whether you identify this guidance as "guardian angels" or know it for what it really is will be a function of your experience and toroidal rotational balance.

When performed properly by a knowledgeable practitioner, hypnotherapy acts as a conduit through the veil that connects you to your higher aspect. The exercises in this book will help you achieve this connection, but a conduit established using hypnotherapy accelerates the process considerably. As you near the end of third density, the pressure of your larger consciousness exerts increasing control upon the decisions that help you choose your path in this lifetime. This directed course has led many to seek a past-life regression without understanding all the benefits that can occur. This is your larger aspect in colorful terms, calling you on the cosmic hotline because you are ready. Whether you pick up the phone or let it ring through is a function of your free will, but the phone will keep ringing.

ENERGETIC BLEED-THROUGH

The veil acts as a cleaning agent to clear your view and allow you an unobstructed perspective of each lifetime. As we have previously stated, there may be some highly charged experiences beyond the veil that still exert an influence upon this lifetime. You may have lived your entire life afraid of something, with no idea why you have this aversion, or you may have an affliction, and doctors cannot identify the cause. These answers are sometimes found within your higher aspect when a connection provides clarity.

Imagine that you had a prior lifetime in which you were a passenger on a ship, traveling on the ocean during a war. The ship was torpedoed while you slept in your berth, and you awoke to water flooding the compartment. Disoriented and panicked, you drowned as the outside force who launched the torpedo forced its will upon you and abruptly ended your incarnation. In this lifetime, you seek a hypnotherapy regression session with a lifelong fear of boats and water and no clear reason for the phobia. During your session, you will be given the answer in one manner or another. If you ask the question, it will be given to you directly. If you do not, you will be shown what happened in the prior lifetime as an observer, allowing you to understand and reconcile the imbalance. This is an example of an energetic steering current that needs to be rebalanced. Let us provide another example as it relates to a medical condition.

In another lifetime, your incarnation was cut short as you were unjustly hanged by your neck for a crime you did not commit. This was not a proper hanging, where your neck was quickly broken, but a traumatic death, where you hung from the rope as it asphyxiated you. Again, an outside influence abruptly ended your incarnation and left the lessons of that life unfinished. You arrive at your session having trouble sleeping because of sleep apnea. You are not overweight, and your doctor cannot find a definitive cause for this affliction, but it exists, and you are living with it. During the session, you will once again observe what occurred in the past life that is energetically bleeding through the veil into this lifetime, and you will reconcile the imbalance.

In both examples above, your higher aspect was engaged and provided the answers that you needed to understand and correct the issues troubling you in this lifetime. How the corrections manifest is up to the individual. A lifelong fear of boats and water is unlikely to be corrected immediately by knowing the initiating factor was your death by drowning in a prior lifetime. What is more likely to occur is that the information may help you establish a basis to rationalize a slow dissolution of the fear as you gain confidence to "test the waters." Energetic bleed-through that causes disorders such as sleep apnea can be corrected during a single session, but it is up to the client and his or her acceptance of the healing.

As the connection is established to the part of your consciousness that exists beyond your veil, an energetic tether is established that will remain after your session. As with any exercise, repetition strengthens and creates muscle memory. Now that you know what it feels like and have experienced it, it will become almost second nature the more you practice connecting in quiet mindfulness.

UNLOCKING THE PURPOSE OF FRAGMENTED CONSCIOUSNESS

We have discussed the concept of ascended fragments incarnating on Earth for their individual purposes. Regardless of what density of consciousness you are a fragment of, you agreed to incarnate on Earth under the veil of forgetfulness. As you made this decision, you were still connected to the knowledge contained within your totality of consciousness, and awakening to your purpose may have seemed like an easy task. However, it is easy to become distracted on Earth and lose sight of your intended mission, especially if you come from a collective that has never experienced polarity or separation. Whether you awaken to your higher purpose or remain locked in ego programming becomes a factor of how much energy can be pushed through the veil to correct your course. The quickest way to affect a course correction is to compel the fragment to seek a qualified hypnotherapist who can break through the veil and connect you to your higher-density aspect. When this happens, the realignment is quick, and the results border on miraculous.

The rules governing this planetary construct require that consciousness awakens to the point where it can ask the proper questions. Consider the multitude of collectives that exist throughout the densities in the cosmos. From these infinite perspectives comes the information to awaken a sleeping planet. Since the higher aspect of these volunteers is a portion of a greater collective, the information they receive will originate from the totality of the body of knowledge that collective contains. Their missions to Earth are to assist in the ascension into fourth density and the ending of polarity and its manifestations. For this reason, you can expect the messages to contain concepts related to acceptance, love, and unity of all creation. There is no redundancy in the messages provided, as all viewpoints of these concepts are required and assist in providing a dimensional perspective of these universal truths.

Self-Healing through Hypnotherapy

Your consciousness contains the energy template of your perfected self. We have provided exercises that will help you realign your body to its energetic perfection through repeated effort. During a session, the connection to the totality of your consciousness allows a clear path for the template to realign the structure of your body. You consciously decided to have the session and have given permission to emerge from separation and return to totality. This allows your consciousness to overlay the energetic template upon your body and use all its resources to correct any imbalances that it identifies in a single treatment. The exercises provided then become a method to maintain the realignment.

Through your successive lifetimes, you have created an energetic template of what you expect to manifest as the vehicle for your incarnation. This template exists within the totality of your consciousness, and the influence it provides during your lifetime depends upon your connection to it. During a session your consciousness will place this golden energy over your body as it exists in its current state. When requested, your consciousness will scan your body and look for differences between the template and your body. The realignment required will depend on the connection you have maintained up to that point and the toxins to which your body has been exposed. Differences between the template and your body will appear as dark spots within the template, where the body has strayed from its blueprint. Using creational energy, your consciousness realigns the darker areas until they once again match the template. In this way the imperfections of the body are realigned and repaired. This is not magic or miracles; it is energy manipulating matter. Your body is matter being coalesced within the sphere of your consciousness. You are merely correcting the deficiencies that have occurred while you operated in separation from your energetic connection.

CHAPTER TWENTY-FOUR
PARTING THOUGHTS

The information in this book provides ascending consciousness with a greater understanding of the cosmos and your relationship within it. As your view expands, you begin to see the interrelationships that exist, and you can no longer wrap yourself in the blanket of separation. Your consciousness is an integral part of the energy balance of this galaxy and the universe. As the galaxy continues along the path of continued energy expansion, Earth must emerge from the experiment of polarity and separation and join the ascending collectives. Like a child who discards the toys that no longer serve them, you must discard the instinctual response of fear and put down your destructive tendencies toward others. This is a prerequisite to ascension and is required to harness the creational energies of God Source. As the name implies, creational energy is used to create. It is harnessed and wielded by those in unity with positivity and love for all things. The assistance provided to Earth and this galaxy to help it emerge from polarity is unprecedented. This assistance currently remains invisible to the masses, but that will change as you continue to discard separation and embrace unity.

The space-time construct that you are embodied within is approaching a deflection point, where ascending consciousness will once again diverge from the current third-density timeline. As previously described, this has happened many times, as the current era remains active and the new era begins. This divergence is different because you will move into fourth density during your incarnations as you co-create your new reality within the ascending collective.

To move with the divergence, you must have the density and rotational balance to do so. You must consciously seek the imbalances within you and release them. Everyone you see is exactly like you, regardless of their embodiment or ascension level. We are all consciousness created from the same photons, gaining the energies of experience. A tree, an insect, a cow, and every human on the planet are composed of the same ingredients. Ascension requires that you awaken from your imagined separations and embrace the higher-order concepts of unity consciousness. A large portion of consciousness currently embodied on Earth acquired the density for ascension long ago. They remained caught in the polarities that existed here and were repeatedly distracted, unaware they were anything more than their ego programming. The information provided in this book and others is a collaborative effort to awaken all whose paths lead them to the knowledge they contain.

The world in which you currently find yourself has structures in place to hinder your awakening and place obstacles along your path. Some were intentional, some were not, but all were created through the manifestations of self-interest. You must identify and discard the teachings that no longer serve you. Clearing your vision is a slow and deliberate process that is unique to each consciousness, but as your vision clears, you will dissolve the structures that obscure higher understandings. Ultimately, you set the intention to move beyond these constructs. One new concept will build upon the other, and your expansion will accelerate as you seek deeper concepts and higher perspectives. When you collect the information that resonates within your consciousness, a light will shine from within and dissipate the amnesia that has obscured your path. As the fog abates, you will see that you are standing on the pinnacle of a mountain. You will feel the balance of your consciousness from within, and you must trust that you will be led in the direction that takes you to your next lesson. As you trust, the next step of your journey will appear. You must take the step, confident that you will be supported.

This is the creation of your reality through the intention of your consciousness. The only limitation is the one you impose upon yourself.

Glossary of Terms

....

- ascend/ascension: The process of expanding conscious density and balancing the resulting oscillating wavelengths. Acquired through repeated experiences that provide a totality of perspective. This balances the rotational geometry, expands the universal aspect ratio, and allows access to higher-order energies.
- awakening: The pressure exerted upon the ego (operative consciousness) to break free from the social paradigm. This occurs when the toroidal geometry of the higher self/aspect that exists beyond the veil of forgetfulness attains the proper rotational balance.
- barrier membrane: The magnetic envelope created around individualized consciousness through the energetic oscillation of photons. This barrier protects the integrity of the unique oscillating energies contained within it.
- channel: Consciousness acting as a willing connection to a source of consciousness other than its own.
- collective: An assembly of consciousnesses operating in sympathetic resonant unity. In lower densities, this manifests as collective intention within a group of individuals. In higher densities, this manifests as collective consciousness.
- collective consciousness: A rotating toroidal sphere comprised of organic consciousness spheres that have ascended beyond the need for the growth and balancing experiences of embodiment (see Figure 9).
- consciousness: An assembly of photons containing the energies of experience that create a unique barrier membrane and energetic wavelength.
- consciousness photon: The base element of the universe from which all else is created. It is the originating component of individualized consciousness when a barrier membrane has been established.
- consciousness wavelength: The unique electromagnetic sine wave emanation generated through photonic oscillations and the resulting angular poloidal rotation. This oscillation occurs within individualized consciousness through the attractive and repulsive forces created within photons as they gain experiential energy.

- cosmos: The material universe to include all space-time constructs, all individualized consciousness, and all collectives of consciousness that exist within the photonic consciousness of God Source.
- creational energy: The default energy that exists within the photons of the cosmos and is used to solidify material creations and energize consciousness.
- density: The number of photons that an individualized consciousness contains within its barrier membrane.
- dimensions: The orientation of an object within a material construct using three coordinates: length, width, and height. Alternatively used within other awakening publications to describe differing space-time envelopes (e.g., "We are ascending into another dimension").
- duality aspect: The division of spherical consciousness into two smaller spheres that must achieve sympathetic resonance to form a dual toroidal vortex as they rejoin during upper fourth density and enter the collective (see Figure 7).
- electromagnetic repulsion: the energetic wavelengths of experience contained within individual photons that push them apart and create oscillations as it acts against the forces of photonic adhesion.
- etheric: the energy constructs manifested within the creational energy interface of collective-consciousness spheres as they manipulate the creational energy of the cosmos (see Figure 9).
- expansion: The process by which consciousness increases photonic density and the energy it contains as it seeks rotational balance and increasing diameter. The ultimate objective of all consciousness.
- first density: The originating density of organic consciousness created from a single photon that subsequently grows and ascends through the experience of existence within material constructs.
- fragment/fragmentation: The sequestering of excess density within ascended consciousness, where a secondary autonomous self-awareness is created and then sent to experience. Used by consciousness that has ascended beyond embodiment to continue to play and assist in the games of experience.
- frequency: The rate at which a photon rotates upon its axis that subsequently determines the velocity of angular rotation within the toroidal sphere of individualized consciousness (see Figure 6).
- galactic consciousness/construct: Fully energized consciousness directly immersed in creational energy. Responsible for the material space-time

constructs within them that have been created for the cultivation of organic consciousness and the enjoyment of all.

- God Source/Source: The consciousness within which the cosmos exists. The center of which (seat of consciousness) is the ultimate donor of all photonic consciousness and acts as the repository for unlimited creational energy.
- higher aspect/self: The portion of the consciousness sphere that exists beyond the veil of forgetfulness that can be accessed during meditation, regression, or at the end of an incarnation. Not to be confused with the perspective of totality of consciousness when dealing with a consciousness fragment.
- light chamber: An etheric device created within the energy of an ascended collective used to realign negative polarity accumulating in consciousness before it reaches levels that cause mutated behaviors.
- operative consciousness: The portion of the toroidal sphere that has been surrounded by an energetic barrier (veil of forgetfulness), which then observes itself as devoid of prior knowledge. The resulting awareness that forms inside the barrier develops within the social paradigm of the construct and gains balancing lessons, unimpeded. Alternately known as ego consciousness.
- organic consciousness: Any consciousness that originated as a single first-density photon within a material construct and ascends through embodiment.
- photonic adhesion: The attraction between photons that causes them to adhere and form groups. When observed within material constructs, it is the attractive force that binds the smallest observable particles and ultimately creates the material constructs of embodiment. Photons and the adhesions inherent within them are the foundation upon which all else is constructed (see Figure 8).
- photonic division: The process by which a single photon divides when energetic saturation causes the resonant frequencies of fracture harmonics. The single photon fractures under the resonance and becomes two smaller particles (see Figure 4).
- photonic spin: The rotational movement of a single photon about its axis that is induced and accelerated through the acquisition of the energy of experience. This is the main component of the term frequency (see Figure 3).

- planetary consciousness: The originating consciousness of the ensuing collective that will ascend through the densities of that material construct. Tasked with maintaining the integrity of the construct and donating the photons required for first-density consciousness.
- polarity—negative: An energetic creation of this galaxy that induces a clockwise rotational photonic spin designed to absorb and cancel polarity—positive as it is acquired by consciousness. Intended to be a minor impediment that induces the forming of collectives to overcome it. In large doses, it causes extreme mutations of conscious intent as the connection to creational energy is lost.
- polarity—positive: The foundational creation energy of the cosmos in which all else exists. This is the energy expected to be acquired by consciousness through experience; it induces a counter-clockwise rotational photonic spin. It does not require an opposing force to exist or to maintain relevance. It is identified as positive within this galaxy to differentiate it from the opposing creation, polarity—negative.
- poloidal: The radial movement of photons within a toroidal sphere that results from electromagnetic oscillations induced through the energy of experience. This can be envisioned as moving up the center column, around and down the outside periphery of the sphere, and back up into the column from below to repeat the process (see Figure 6).
- QHHT: Quantum healing hypnosis technique is a scripted form of hypnotic regression pioneered by Dolores Cannon that allows a client's higher self to select past-life memories and then question it to discuss the relevance of what was shown.
- realignment: The act of changing/overpowering the oscillating wavelength of consciousness photons. Used to create self-aware fragments or to clear nonbeneficial experiential energy.
- resonant frequency: The oscillation of a photon within consciousness that causes it to become unstable and divide. Caused as the photon reaches energetic saturation, which raises the frequency of spin and amplitude of vibration to the fracture point (see Figure 4).
- resonate: The sympathetic electromagnetic oscillation of wavelengths between individualized consciousnesses. When two consciousness wavelength frequencies are at the same pitch and tempo, they create a harmonic vibration that increases in amplitude and can be felt as an internal empowerment. This is the foundational requirement of collective consciousness.

- seat of consciousness: The self-actualized center of the toroidal column, where the perspective of self-awareness is generated in individualized consciousness. This is also where the veil-of-forgetfulness partition is erected.
- second density: The requisite number of photons within a consciousness to induce a simplistic rotating toroidal architecture. The center column has not formed, and the self-aware seat of consciousness has not fully developed (see Figure 5).
- space-time: Any four-dimensional material construct created within a gravitational lock. Used for the creation, ascension, and enjoyment of consciousness. Presented by Albert Einstein in 1905 in his work "On the Electrodynamics of Moving Bodies" and furthered by Hermann Minkowski in 1908.
- system consciousness: The consciousness responsible for the subsequent planetary spheres that will exist within it. The creational energy interface at the center of its toroidal column is where the visible energy generator will reside. The energy is modified and filtered commensurate with the requirements of the intended life-forms.
- third density: The requisite number of consciousness photons that contain the required energy of experience to create the toroidal column and rotation of a self-actualized seat of consciousness.
- timeline: The perception of a linear chronology of past events and future probabilities from any perspective within a gravitational space-time construct.
- time-space: The observation of existence of a self-aware consciousness in the ever present now of the cosmos, when not interacting in a material gravitational construct.
- toroidal sphere: The rotating geometry of all self-aware consciousness that resembles a doughnut. Created through the attraction, repulsion, and spin rate of photons as they oscillate and rotate in an angular poloidal rotation within the sphere (see Figure 6).
- totality of consciousness: The entire photonic array of an individualized consciousness at any location within the cosmos, regardless of fragmentation or compartmentalization. The photons oscillate at a wavelength unique to the consciousness and are accessible through meditation and focus.
- triad of light: The graphic representation of the growth of consciousness and a meditative tool used to visualize its expansion (see book cover).

- travelers: Small pockets of consciousness that exist within a third-density toroidal sphere. Created through repeated, obsessive focus upon an event or person.
- twin flame: A colorful term for duality aspect.
- universal aspect ratio: As referenced in the triad of light, The ratio between the diameter of the funnel openings, the length of the column between them, and the equatorial diameter of a toroidal sphere of a self-aware consciousness. The aspect ratio is then applied to the mathematical sequence 3, 6, and 9 which produces the optimum photonic spacing intervals of a perfectly balanced geometric sphere for the given ratio.
- veil of forgetfulness: An energetic barrier erected within individual consciousness that separates the operative consciousness from the remaining portion of the toroidal sphere. Erected at the periphery of the seat of consciousness (see Figure 6).
- vibration: The oscillation of photons within consciousness that results from the acquisition of experiential energy.
- we: The twelve originating galactic consciousnesses of this cosmos that provide the information to the readers of the book.
- you: The ascending consciousnesses engaging with this text.

References/Additional Reading

1. https://www.dolorescannon.com/about-qhht.
2. D. Salart, A. Baas, C. Branciard, N. Gisin, H. Zbinden, "Testing Spooky Action at a Distance" (Aug. 25, 2008), https://arxiv.org/abs/0808.3316.
3. Burra G. Sidharth, "Comments on the Mass of the Photon," https://arxiv.org/abs/physics/0607208.
4. Burra G. Sidharth, "On the Photon Mass" (June 22, 2007), https://arxiv.org/abs/0706.3319.
5. Y. Liu, Y. Ke, H. Luo, et al. "Photonic Spin Hall Effect in Metasurfaces: a Brief Review," *Nanophotonics* 6, no. 1 (2016): 51–70, https://www.degruyter.com/view/j/nanoph.2017.6.issue-1/nanoph-2015-0155/nanoph-2015-0155.xml.
6. "The Dark Energy Survey: more than dark energy—an overview," The Dark Energy Survey Collaboration (Aug. 19, 2016), https://arxiv.org/abs/1601.00329.
7. https://science.nasa.gov/astrophysics/focus-areas/what-is-dark-energy.
8. Andrea Amoretti, Daniel Arean, Riccardo Argurio, Daniele Musso, Leopoldo A. Pando Zayas, "A holographic perspective on phonons and pseudo-phonons" (May 9. 2017), https://arxiv.org/abs/1611.09344.
9. M. T. Dove, "Introduction to the Theory of Lattice Dynamics," Department of Earth Sciences, University of Cambridge, https://doi.org/10.1051/sfn/201112007.
10. B. J. Holzer, "Introduction to Particle Accelerators and Their Limitations" (May 26, 2017), https://arxiv.org/abs/1705.09601.
11. Richard Nisius, "The Structure of Quasi-Real and Virtual Photons," (July 10, 1999), https://arxiv.org/abs/hep-ex/9907012.
12. "Searches for Lepton Number Violation and Resonances in $K_\pm \rightarrow \pi\mu\mu$ Decays" (Mar 22, 2017), https://arxiv.org/abs/1612.04723.
13. Albert Einstein, "On the Electrodynamics of Moving Bodies" (June 30, 1905), http://www.fourmilab.ch/etexts/einstein/specrel/www.
14. Hermann Minkowski Space-Time Overview, https://en.wikipedia.org/wiki/Minkowski_space.

ABOUT THE AUTHOR

TODD DEVINEY is a regression therapist and intuitive empath who was born the youngest of three in Miami Florida. His working career began directly after high school as a mechanic in the United States Navy. After an honorable discharge he continued his education and obtained a federal license to operate commercial nuclear reactors. This led to the creation of a consulting firm that contracted with nuclear plants around the United States.

Successful but unsatisfied with walking the well trodden path of an accepted life, he began searching for inner fulfillment. After a few false starts and some painful lessons, his inner work culminated in a desire to help others. However, before the ability to help others can manifest you must first help yourself. That help came on 11/11 at 11 AM during a QHHT regression session where Todd experienced an energetic upgrade, or what is often referred to as a Kundalini Awakening. This has left him with the ability of 'second sight' and a connection to a higher awareness.

Due to the profound changes that have occurred in his life since that session, he became a certified regression therapist to provide the experience to others. The altruistic nature of this work is reinforced through the messages received from clients long after their sessions have finished.

Todd currently lives with his wife and daughter in North Carolina with two dogs, four chickens, and six fish. He has a regression therapy practice, posts articles on the internet, and lectures when time permits as he attempts to share what he has received with others.

You can listen to clips from client sessions who have allowed interesting portions of their sessions to be posted, and clips where Todd is the client answering questions about consciousness and our collective future at; YouTube: Enlightened Aspect Productions.

To contact Todd for a session or to ask a question visit the website, EnlightenedAspectProductions.org or Email, Enlightenedaspectproductions@gmail.com

Printed in the United States
By Bookmasters